THE ARTIST'S DAUGHTER

A MEMOIR

ALEXANDRA KUYKENDALL

a division of Baker Publishing Group
Grand Rapids, Michigan

Published by Revell
a division of Baker Publishing Group
P.O. Box 6287, Grand Rapids, MI 49516-6287
www.revellbooks.com

Printed in the United States of America

Library of Congress Cataloging-in-Publication Data is on file at the Library of Congress, Washington, DC.

ISBN 978-0-8007-2205-0 (pbk.)

Published in association with the literary agency of Alive Communications, Inc., 7680 Goddard Street, Suite 200, Colorado Springs, Colorado 80920, www.alivecommunications.com.

To protect the privacy of those who have shared their stories with the author, some details and names have been changed.

The internet addresses, email addresses, and phone numbers in this book are accurate at the time of publication. They are provided as a resource. Baker Publishing Group does not endorse them or vouch for their content or permanence.

13 14 15 16 17 18 19 7 6 5 4 3 2 1

In keeping with biblical principles of creation stewardship, Baker Publishing Group advocates the responsible use of our natural resources. As a member of the Green Press Initiative, our company uses recycled paper when possible. The text paper of this book is composed in part of post-consumer waste.

For all of my family circles.
You shape my heart each day.
Especially for my mother.
You showed me the world
and gave me your everything.
I am forever grateful.

Contents

Section 10 Fear

Section 11 Ten Days

Section 1

Insecurity

i

Barcelona

July afternoons in Barcelona are hot and still. It was a week before my ninth birthday, and the heat made me, an American girl, want to hide and find relief. To find reprieve from the stifling air, from the questions of who I was and where I came from. There was no escaping any of it as I sat next to my mother in the backseat of the cab while we drove to a designated café. My legs stuck together from the sweat, and I wanted to scratch and squirm. Despite my age, I was good at holding things in, so I willed myself to sit still and pushed my nerves and excitement down, piling them onto the mountain of questions and unease I'd been holding in my entire life. Maybe today would be a new beginning, and the holes from my past would start to fill. I forced my breath out slowly and looked out the window at the tree-lined streets speeding by.

I knew that when we finally arrived and I stepped out of the cab, I needed to present my best self. I'd waited years for this moment and I wanted to be ready. Looking down at my stiff, royal blue and white cotton dress, I smoothed out the wrinkles with sticky palms. I decided again the dress was a good choice for the occasion.

I wanted to be more than beautiful. I wanted to be captivating to the man I was about to meet for the first time: my father.

The cab ride was a splurge; my mother wanted to be on time, and we both wanted to look our best. The splurge allowed us to wear pretty, impractical shoes that wouldn't have worked walking blocks from a subway station. I closed my eyes and took a deep breath. What made my mom look him up in the phone book the day before? Had she been planning on seeing him all along? And why hadn't I known he lived here before we arrived in this city for our vacation?

My mother sat in her sundress next to me, her tanned shoulders hinting at our recent weeks of walking through Italian tourists' sights and sitting on Spanish beaches. She looked straight ahead, and I got the feeling she was remembering another time. I wondered if the landmarks whizzing by looked familiar to her, but I was afraid to ask because I sensed the memories weren't simple—and weren't meant for me. She was my model for holding it together under pressure, and her cues told me now was one of those times. I leaned toward the open window and felt the warm breeze on my face as it blew my hair back. I examined each stone apartment building we passed and wondered if that was where my father lived.

As the taxi pulled up to the curb, my mother looked down at me. She rarely talked about her feelings, but we spent almost every minute together, and I read apprehension in her eyes, then determination to push through the discomfort for my sake. Her eyes asked me, *Are you ready for this?*

Why had she arranged this meeting? Maybe because she thought I had a right to meet my father—or he had a right to meet me. I knew she was proud of me, so maybe she wanted to show me off. Or maybe it was simply because I had been asking more questions the last few years and we were in Barcelona.

She broke our gaze, and I noticed her jaw was tense as she opened her coin purse and deliberately counted out the pesetas for the cab fare. Reaching her arm over the front seat to the driver with an elegance she brought to every gesture, she handed him the coins with an expert "*Gracias.*" Just past her fortieth birthday, she was, without a doubt, a beautiful woman, and even at eight I knew men recognized that.

I peered over her sun-browned shoulder as she paid, expecting to see someone I recognized. A man I was sure would be handsome, probably rugged and tan, definitely tall. I thought he would be standing at the corner waiting for us, but all I saw was an empty sidewalk with the heat rising off it and, in the distance, a café patio covered by a striped fabric awning, creating some shade for the few people scattered at the tables. He probably hadn't arrived yet. Otherwise he'd surely be standing at the corner waiting for us, for me.

My mother slid her long legs out of the car, and I scooted along the vinyl backseat bench of the cab, my dress sticking to the back of my legs as I followed her out the curbside door. I had daydreamed about this moment with increasing frequency the last few years, sure it would be a reunion of Hallmark quality with lots of hugs, laughing, and recognition.

Stepping out of the car, I looked down again at my dress and repeated the smoothing motion with my hands. The colors reminded me of the Dutch tableware that belonged to my babysitter back home in Seattle. And the style reminded me of the Dutch girls painted on the plates and cups. The dress had puffy sleeves, a full skirt, and crisscrossing threads in the front, like a corset, that were pulled tight and tied in a bow. The blue matched the color of my eyes, the eyes that often drew compliments from strangers. The dress was the result of a shopping spree with my mom a few days earlier, and I wore it with expectation.

My mother and I paused at the corner, looking at the café's patio a few doors down, sweat beads forming on our foreheads. It was siesta time, and Barcelona natives were home avoiding the midday heat. The traffic noise was quieted to the occasional buzz of a scooter. Most of the thirty wrought-iron tables in front of us were empty. My mother's hand slid into mine. I followed her silent lead as she walked toward the covered patio. Her arms and gait matched the stiffness I'd noticed in her jaw. I did my own imitation of a royal walk, keeping my chin up and my back straight like a princess entering the ballroom to finally meet her prince.

We were on the tail end of a yearlong adventure. We'd left the United States the summer before to move to Italy, where my mother found a job in a small factory town, teaching English to middle managers of local industries. For a year we lived the expatriate lifestyle, something she was used to from her years of living overseas as an English teacher—but I wasn't. I missed french fries and Saturday morning cartoons and was tired of being the outsiders in a small town that didn't see many of them. So together we decided to move back to Seattle and call our adventure quits. On our way home, we stopped in Barcelona for a month to visit the friends my mom had made in the four years she'd lived there: two years before my birth and two after.

As we approached the café patio, my eyes quickly moved across the group of tables, assessing the few patrons seated outside. I was only interested in the men and quickly sized up each one. Some were sitting with women, their conversations hushed. Only a handful of the male customers were seated alone, and none of them jumped out as the man in waiting.

"There he is," my mom said in almost a whisper, barely moving her lips. I thought she must be wrong, because I'd already searched the tables and didn't see anyone who could be my father.

An old man stood up. He was looking at us, smiling, but I was sure he couldn't be my father. He had whitish-gray hair, long in the back, and his long-sleeved dress shirt and pants were wrinkled, like he had slept in them the night before. He looked like an aged, disheveled hippy, and I felt disappointment take over. In my mind, dads were in their midthirties with business suits and clean-cut hair, like models in the JCPenney catalog.

The old man waved at my mom, and despite my desire for a younger, more chiseled version, she gave a small wave back. This couldn't be right. This couldn't be the man I had wondered about the last few years, who I'd drawn pictures for with his first name written across the top. Who I'd hoped would love me so much when he saw me that he would not let any more years go by without me.

Before I could convince my mother otherwise, we floated toward his table and sat down across from him. He and my mother gave the customary European quick kiss on each cheek. He sat down, stared at me, and smiled. The butterflies in my stomach had changed to running mountain goats. I looked away, not sure what the next step in the process should be. My daydreams about this moment hadn't included awkwardness. I looked down at his hands resting on the table. There were age spots on them.

"Would you like something to drink?" he asked me in English that carried a heavy accent. I looked at my mother for permission, and she gave a slight nod, indicating to go ahead and order whatever I wanted. I was thirsty from the heat but knew a Coke would come in a bottle half the size of the United States version, and without ice. Even though a Coke sounded refreshing, I didn't want to be disappointed by the two-sip-sized soda.

"A Yoo-hoo, please," I answered. I knew the chocolate milk in a bottle would be more and I could make it last longer.

When the young waitress returned to put our drinks on the table, the old man spoke with her in a language I didn't understand. She laughed at his words with a familiarity. Was it because he knew her, or was he just flirtatious? Was this his regular spot? If so, was she wondering who I was?

I took small sips of my chocolate drink, trying to make it last as long as possible as my mom made small talk with this foreigner.

She explained our year in Italy. I knew the story well—she wanted me to learn a second language and figured soon I would be too old to learn one quickly. And now we were headed back to Seattle.

"We're only in Barcelona two more weeks," she said, making it clear this was a short-term visit.

My Yoo-hoo tasted cool and thick and sweet, but already I knew it wasn't enough. Just like the man sitting across the table from me. I already felt he wasn't enough. Not what I had in mind when I ordered a father. I'd waited so long, it seemed doubly unfair that now I would have to get the secondhand model.

He leaned toward me from across the table and picked up one of my hands and turned it over in his. His fingers were long, with dirt under the fingernails. As he touched my hand, his skin felt soft and wrinkled. A shiver went through me and I started feeling more anxious. I wanted to leave.

"Your fingers, they are long," he said with pride. I didn't answer, not sure what the proper response was. "Thank you" didn't seem right. Out of the corner of my eye, I could see my mother's excellent posture.

His gaze moved from the top of my head down and across my face from ear to ear. He was searching me. Did he need, as I did, to find something familiar in the person in front of him?

"Your eyes. They're so blue," he said. No surprise. A remark I often got at first meetings. Then he said something I will never forget. "They look just like my mother's." He paused as though recognizing the weight of his comment. It was heavy with innuendo about genetics and generations and what should be and what wasn't. His mother, my grandmother. Her eyes, mine. A relationship that should be sacred was nonexistent.

"Her birthday is next week," my mother reminded him. "She'll be nine." Another indicator that things weren't as they should be. How would a father not know his own child's birthday? It's as if he needed to be reminded of my very existence.

He reached out and touched me with tender, stroking motions—my arm, my hair, my face. I looked up at the canvas awning, down at the table, over his shoulder into the restaurant. I didn't want to be impolite, but he seemed to be asking me for something I couldn't give.

When it was time to go, we all stood up, and he put his arm around my shoulder and squeezed from the side. The hug felt uncomfortable, unfamiliar, and forced, not what I thought my father would feel like. I thought there would be a familiarity with this man. I was disappointed there wasn't. But I couldn't help being hopeful—a long-held habit. Maybe when the awkwardness passed, when he knew me, I would know what it was to have a father's love. That gaping hole would be filled.

ii

ITALY

We were a pair of traveling adventurers, my mother and I. We spent my first birthday on Crete. We watched the New York Harbor from the Statue of Liberty's crown when I was five. We walked through the ruins of Mount Vesuvius in Naples when I was eight. And now we were headed back to home base, the Pacific Northwest. Every daughter looks to her mother to see what a woman is supposed to be. I knew mine was unique. Independent. Traveled. Confident. Beautiful. I saw those qualities in me because I saw them in her.

Right before my second birthday, we left Barcelona for an island off Seattle. We arrived in America just in time to celebrate the country's bicentennial. My mom has a picture of me on a rocky beach, standing next to a piece of driftwood, waving a little American flag on a stick and wearing all red, white, and blue.

A few of our years on the island, we lived with a man I called Daddy. When he decided he didn't want a ready-made family, he left, confirming the title Daddy meant "one who abandons." His breakup with my mother was also his breakup with me. It was then I started asking my mother about my "real father," and she told me his foreign name. Until our meeting at the café, the only thing I remember knowing about my father was his first name. It surprised me. I didn't know anyone with that name. I was just learning to write, and I wrote it in crayon across the top of my pictures.

After the man I'd called Daddy left, my mother decided a fresh start was in order. We started making plans to go to Europe. A year before that hot Barcelona afternoon, my mother and I arrived in Rome with two one-way tickets and five maroon and navy suitcases, a matching set she bought for our adventure. The suitcases ranged in size from extra-large to tiny and made me feel like we were going on a safari. My mother figured she'd find a job when we arrived in the country. That's how she'd always done it.

"Do you all have a place to stay tonight?" a talkative woman sitting across the airplane aisle from my mother asked. "I have a reservation at a *pensione* at the top of the Spanish Steps, if you want to share it."

"Okay," my mother replied without appearing to give it much thought.

I looked up from my Nancy Drew book in surprise. "We don't even know her," I whispered to my mom as the plane was descending.

"That's what you do when you're traveling. Rome is expensive. This will cut our night's stay in half."

When our cab pulled up to the *pensione*, I saw a white stone staircase the width of three buildings and the length of a block cascading down to a street below: the Spanish Steps. The three of us stepped into the reserved room, felt the stale air push against us, and found only one bed.

The chatty stranger turned to me. "Let's go up to the rooftop and sleep. It'll be cooler up there." Obviously an extrovert, she figured an eight-year-old was better than no company at all.

"I'm not so sure," my mother answered. Sharing a room with a stranger was one thing, having her take her eight-year-old daughter alone to the roof was another. Besides, my mother had warned me not to be the "ugly American," an obnoxious person who showed up in a different country and demanded to know why no one did things like they do back home. "You want to blend in," my mother said. I knew the look she was giving meant she doubted this woman was very good at blending in.

"Please, Mommy! I'm not even tired."

My mother made a comment about jet lag, and I decided it was permission. So the stranger woman and I took blankets and pillows up to the rooftop patio and laid them on top of cushions from the patio furniture. We listened to the traffic of scooters buzzing and honking through the night as our bodies fought the idea of sleep in a new time zone. My mom kept coming up to check on me, but I wanted to stay with the talker.

The next morning my mom and I sat at a little table on the same rooftop, where breakfast was being served. It was included in the price of the room, so we weren't going to miss it.

"Where are the pancakes?" I asked.

"Here, try these," my mother said, pointing to the words *fresh figs* on the menu. "It's fruit."

"I want pancakes. Where are the pancakes?"

"Here, have some bread and cheese." She pointed to another item on the paper.

"I'm hungry. I want a *real* breakfast." I was not going to be tricked into believing that bread and cheese was breakfast. "Is there any cereal?"

"This is breakfast in Italy."

I wasn't sure about Italy.

From bustling Rome we boarded a creaking train and headed to towns pulled from my mother's memory, places she'd visited when she was younger. Our cash reserves were sparse and the school year was starting soon, so the need for a job was growing urgent.

I watched from the train windows as countryside and beach sped by, a blur of sun, water, and sparkles. Farms that looked like places I'd only seen in picture books, old women dressed all in black, and chickens running across dirt streets.

At each new town, my mom scanned the phone book for private language schools and placed a cold call, offering her services as an experienced teacher of English as a second language. Her résumé included years in Peru, Barcelona, New York City, and most recently Seattle, where she taught refugees from Africa and Asia to speak the language of their new rainy home. She was no college student backpacking through Europe. She was a professional, with a master's degree in ESL and a child to support.

We quickly developed a system for boarding the trains. The second-class cars were the Southwest Airlines of Italian travel, with people waiting in line outside the train doors and scrambling to find seats once they opened. Small and quick, I was able to squirm past the grown-up-sized bodies and suitcases and, if lucky, find two seats together. Then I would lay my body across both seats and avoid eye contact with the Italians, who were annoyed they'd been outpushed by a foreign child. My mother followed, her arms overflowing with our five matching suitcases. When we didn't get seats, we were crammed in the walkway, sitting on the bigger bags, trying to catch a breeze from the open windows.

The small factory town we landed in was not the picturesque village my mom envisioned when we started on our Italian trek. Terni is nestled between Florence and Rome in the region of Umbria, which is famous for its hill towns: Perugia, Todi, Assisi. Towns surrounded by stone walls built to protect them in medieval times and perched on hills with centuries of history at every step. But Terni, a major train-switching spot, had been bombed during World War II. *Quaint* and *historic* were replaced with high-rise apartments from the sixties and seventies. It was our landing spot because, not surprisingly, no other Americans wanted to live and teach English there. Unlike the postcard-worthy towns, Terni had a job for my mother.

Nearly thirty years later, these stories of my childhood feel disconnected from my life as a married mother of four. My current routines of making school lunches, scheduling around naptimes and church on Sunday, don't match with the continent hopping of my early years. But I think my eight-year-old self would have liked to know where her life was headed, because the downside to adventure is insecurity.

Even as I write these pages, I have a wheezy baby on my lap, home only hours from our latest visit to the emergency room. I have a toddler napping in a crib that she doesn't want to admit she's outgrown, and two reading and writing freckled girls who need to be picked up from school. That eight-year-old girl in Barcelona, that only child, would have been pleased to know that I almost always have a child at arm's reach and my fridge is full of Diet Coke.

iii

Apartment

Before our good-bye at the café, my father had invited us to his apartment the following week for a birthday lunch.

"I will make paella," he said with a confidence I would later call arrogance. "You will like it. I am quite good at it."

My mother nodded. "He is a good cook."

I was surprised she knew this. Why hadn't she ever shared this critical fact before? I had heard almost nothing about my father from her, which made the comment even more surprising, like I was just learning they'd had any kind of relationship. As long as I can remember, my mom was matter-of-fact about the birds and the bees. At nine I knew where babies came from, or at least how they were conceived, but I was still shocked at this familiarity that suggested a relationship. I had never really thought of my father in terms of my mother. And I never really would. My relationship with him would remain separate from her. Theirs was a thing of the past that my mother saw no reason to talk about.

A week after our first meeting, my mother and I stepped into the cool, stone-tiled lobby of my father's eight-story apartment building. The lobby was a modern contrast to the musty castles and dark cathedrals I'd spent the last year touring. We were greeted by a rotund doorman sitting on a stool behind the desk. Other than characters in books and movies, I didn't know anyone who had a doorman and was instantly impressed.

The doorman pushed down on the desk to hoist himself up and escorted us to the elevator. Pulling back the black iron accordion gate, he stepped aside for us to step inside. The antique gate he pulled closed behind us was a reminder that we were still in the Old World. We peered at him through the gate's bars like inmates at a jailor who had just locked their cell. He smiled at us and disappeared from view as the elevator went up. We watched in silence as the floors scrolled past us one by one.

Walking into my father's apartment was like walking into an art gallery. The stark white walls and floors and black leather furniture showcased the artwork displayed on the walls and underfoot. These were not pieces he'd collected from exotic travels; these were ones he'd created with his own long-fingered, age-spotted hands. It turned out the dirt I'd noticed under his fingernails days earlier was actually paint. Paintings in the entry had random objects I recognized protruding from them: razors, women's underwear, satin gloves. Stepping into the living room, I saw tapestries hanging from floor to ceiling. There were no landscapes or women standing next to lakes with parasols—what I pictured when I thought of artwork. More like blobs of fabric and yarn with swirly strands protruding. On the floor were bushy mounds of woven rugs. I wasn't sure if they were meant for walking on.

"This is where I sleep . . . the bathroom . . . the kitchen," he explained as he gave us a quick tour of the apartment. I pictured him eating breakfast at the table in the living room. I wondered what he wore when he sat there. Did he read the newspaper? Drink coffee? Was he alone?

"Let's go downstairs," he said with a twinkle in his eye. "I have something to show you."

He took us down a few floors in the caged elevator to see another apartment, his studio. As we stepped into the huge room, the natural light flooded in from a wall of windows. We stepped around drop cloths and half-completed pieces on the floor as he talked, and his tone became much more animated than it had been upstairs.

"This one," he said as he pointed to a painting on the floor with red and yellow vertical stripes, "has the colors of the Catalan flag." He led us to the second side room dominated by two looms used to create the tapestries he was known for. Spools of yarn taller than me leaned against the walls. The paint fumes hit my nose, and I took a thousand mental pictures.

His voice got more excited with each piece he described. I was impressed and unimpressed at the same time. Impressed because I'd already learned from my mother that his art wasn't just a hobby; my father was well known and respected in Spain. He lived in this upscale apartment building because he sold his work for what appeared to me to be a lot of money. Unimpressed because I wasn't there to see tapestries. I wanted him to turn to me, ignore the loom next to us, and apologize for being silent and absent up to that point. To promise me a new beginning. My mother later said that sharing his art with me was his way of sharing himself. I didn't see it. I wanted something more.

Back in the kitchen, I watched as he chopped onions. Cooking wasn't a talent I'd imagined in my father, but it sat well with me. It sounded domestic, caregiving. On our way to his apartment that day, my mother had explained that paella is a traditional Spanish dish. But as he stirred the rice, he instructed me that this paella was made with seafood because his was a Catalan recipe. He held up a shrimp as proof. From Catalonia, the province that surrounds Barcelona, butting up to the sea and to France.

"We are Catalan, not Spanish," he explained. *We?* He was putting me in a category with himself. I liked it.

"No, we are not Spanish." His face scrunched as he said it, the very thought creating distaste. "Borders. They don't mean anything."

I thought we were in Spain. I was confused, but I listened intently.

"*We* are Catalan. We speak a language no one else in the world speaks."

Years later he would tell me the Mediterranean is the cultural center of the world. "Look at all of the best food, music, and art," he would say. "It comes from the countries that surround the Mediterranean."

Maybe artists are always self-focused, or maybe having people treat you like a celebrity shapes your personality, but I would later see these comments about the center of the world as further evidence of his outlook on where he stood in it.

But standing there in his kitchen, I didn't understand what he was saying. I hung on to every word anyway, hoping for clues to where I fit into the "we," and held my questions in for later pondering. How did I, the bubble-gum-chewing, Muppets-loving, tennis-shoe-wearing American girl fit into this larger "we"?

"We will separate from Spain one day." He nodded as he said it, agreeing with himself. I got the feeling I didn't need to be there for him to have this one-sided conversation.

His eyes suddenly lit up. "I have something to show you!" Wiping his hands on a towel, he walked into the living room and I followed behind. He pulled a large book off the bookshelf. The spine displayed his name in all caps. Opening the book, he quickly flipped through the glossy pages until he found what he was looking for and placed the open book on my lap.

"I made this for you." I looked down to see a photo of a painting with red at the top bleeding down into dark, and in the bottom right-hand corner a small, blonde figure—a child, faceless, with two blue smudges for eyes. He pointed at the title. *Solitut D'Alexandra.*

Alexandra's Solitude. Next to the title was written 1980, the year it was painted. That would have made me six years old. He was thinking about me then, years after we left Barcelona. He was thinking about me being alone. Worried about my solitude. Why didn't he come find me? My soul screamed it as I stared in silence at the picture.

"It will be yours someday," he said. "I'm saving it for you."

Great, I thought. *Just what I want, a painting of me with no face, and I have to wait for you to die to get it.* He looked at me with expectation. I could tell he thought I would be excited.

I was beginning to wonder how this relationship was going to play out. I had come with hopes of trips back and forth across the ocean, of my own spot in his apartment, like kids I knew with divorced parents who had some things at their dad's place. I dreamed of going to art shows and museums with him and being introduced as the artist's daughter. Of him taking me shopping, buying me outfits and toys, not in the discount basements of the department stores like where my mom and I shopped, but in the Daddy Warbucks kind of way, with the entire store's staff attending to me while dancing a choreographed routine.

My hopes morphed quickly into fantasies that I knew wouldn't come true. It was safer that way—to keep my thoughts on the impossible. I'd be less likely to be disappointed when they didn't happen.

iv

ZOO

A few days later my mother and I met my father at the zoo. This was now our third meeting and I was still waiting for the familiarity to kick in. I watched as my father greeted the other invitee to our outing: his adult daughter, my half sister. Tall like my mother, she gave him two quick kisses on the cheek and laughed as she rested her hand on his arm, speaking to him in Catalan. She flashed my mother a warm smile, and they exchanged an awkward handshake. Then she turned to me, her smile broadening. I instantly liked her, even though there was nothing about her that made me think of a sister. She was in her twenties and lived with her boyfriend. She probably wasn't interested in Nancy Drew or Chinese jump rope.

She bent down so we were looking eye to eye. We did the same thing I did with our father at first meeting—searched each other for something familiar, something that confirmed that we were tied together. I couldn't say anything if I'd wanted to. She spoke Spanish and Catalan. I spoke English and Italian. The language barrier freed us to simply look and smile while the monkeys squawked in the background.

Watching my sister with our father, I knew she had something I wanted. She had a familiarity with him that only time together could create. Even if everything changed that day, I knew she would always have more years with him than I did. And I knew she had a brother. I saw pictures in our father's apartment of the two of them together. A brother. *I* had a brother. If you define a sibling as someone who is connected to you by blood only.

My sister pulled a little cloth doll out of her purse. It had a purple dress, yarn for hair, and could fit in my hand. We took turns walking the doll up each other's arms, making it dance, giving it movement that didn't require real dialogue. We connected without words, and when it was time to say good-bye, she told me through our father that she couldn't give me the doll; she needed to keep it because her mother had given it to her as a gift. I felt a tinge of irrational jealousy. Was I surprised she had a mother? Of course not, I knew how these things worked. In fact, her mother had a son my age with another man. More tinges of confusing jealousy. Apparently both her parents had moved on by the time I was conceived. It was further confirmation that our family was complicated. And with complication comes more complication.

Hugging her good-bye, I didn't know where I fit into my father's and sister's lives. Things for her would not change after the zoo. She would go back to meeting her friends for tapas, studying psychology, and joining our father for lunch. But I wanted to believe that things for me, for us, would change. She wasn't what I had pictured in a sister, but I would take it. Really, why would this twentysomething woman need to have a relationship with me? I didn't offer her much more than a reminder that her father was a little reckless and irresponsible.

A few days later, my mother and I packed up our matching luggage and boarded a plane back to Seattle. She had a job waiting in Seattle, and the school year was starting. As the plane landed at

Sea-Tac Airport, the evergreen trees outside the tiny window and the cool, damp air felt wonderfully familiar. My mother rented a furnished apartment on Capitol Hill and began looking for a house to buy. I didn't think of it at the time, but buying a house meant the nomadic life was over. No more fresh starts.

One day when we were in the apartment, something triggered a wave of emotion that came out all screamy and angry.

"Why doesn't he write? Why doesn't he call? I hate him!" I yelled at my mom.

I kicked the sofa and ran into the bedroom. I threw a pillow on the floor. And then another. I picked them both up and threw them as hard as I could at the wall. I felt the anger in my legs, arms, fingertips. It wanted to burst open, and I was confused by it.

My mom came running in after me, giving me what I wanted: someone's attention. But really, her attention was something I already had. I wanted his.

"I don't know. Calm down," she pleaded.

"I don't wanna calm down!"

That was true. The crack had been forced open when I met my father face-to-face. The color of my eyes and the dark circles under them were a reflection of his. I saw them, him, every time I looked in the mirror. I couldn't overlook the reality that had been steeping for nine years. My father was ignoring me. And now, after he'd met me, the sting was worse. He now knew what he was missing. And he still chose to stay away.

I ran back in the living room, looking around for something safe to hit without really being destructive. Even in that moment I wanted to be responsible, to hold it all in. But the hurt was leaking out with increasing intensity. It was so different from my controlled behavior that it felt scary and great at the same time. My mom tried wrapping her arms around me. I pushed out of them. I wasn't ready to be comforted. I wanted to be angry. Didn't I have the right to be angry?

The anger quickly moved to grief. And the sobs came out in bellows. A childhood's worth of confusion and abandonment raced out like an exorcism, and though I didn't like feeling out of control, I wanted to let out what had been trapped in my chest for so long.

Finally, exhausted, I leaned into my mother and let her do what she'd wanted to the last twenty minutes. She wrapped her long arms around me and rocked her baby. She used her hand to wipe the tears from my face. We both knew it was the most she could do.

For all of the holding tightly my mother did, I was created to be loved, to be held, by two parents. No matter how much she loved me, she couldn't be my father too. I was left flailing, insecure, wanting something more.

Section 2

Love Is a Choice

i

Jesus

"So, what do you think?" Michelle asked. "Who was Jesus?"

I leaned against the wood-paneled wall, squeezed between two other high school girls in the top bunk, and waited for someone else to answer first. Our room for the weekend retreat was only wide enough for a row of bunk beds on each side and a walkway down the middle. It was our second night at Breakaway Lodge on the Oregon Coast. Damp, sandy socks and windbreakers spilled out of duffle bags, creating a continuous pile of laundry ready to go home. All of the girls from our West Seattle group squeezed together on the top bunks so we could see each other for our "cabin time" talk.

For the last six months, Michelle and Gretchen, two women in their twenties, offered fun in the midst of my fourteen-year-old hormonal mood swings and lack of transportation. They took me to high school football games and planned pizza nights. They were volunteers with a group called Young Life. Jolene, a junior and a teacher's assistant in my freshman health class, invited a group of my freshmen friends to one of Young Life's Monday night clubs. "You have so much fun, you don't even need to drink," Jolene told us when the teacher was out of the room. I figured that was good since I was a rule follower. That night, I walked to meet Jolene in my high school's parking lot and climbed into Gretchen's car for a scavenger hunt.

Michelle, a newlywed attorney, brought the courtroom shock factor into every conversation by inserting "always" and "never" statements when talking about life. "Never have sex before you're married." "Always read your Bible in the morning." At twenty-eight, she was a legit grown-up who I suspected used this language of extremes to get high schoolers riled up and talking too. Talking about boys and sex, drinking and Jesus.

Gretchen was all bones and big eyes that peered out from her dark hair. Having graduated from college only a few months before we met, she spent her sparse extra dollars from her first teaching job to take me to the movies. Michelle pushed and Gretchen explained.

They told me about Jesus, how he was God in human form, and that's why we celebrate his birth at Christmas. And the most shocking part—what the cross was all about. How he was nailed to it so I could be reconciled with God, so we all could. I had no idea there was a purpose behind his death and asked lots of questions. I'd spent my childhood walking through my fair share of musty European cathedrals. I'd seen many a crucifix with blood dripping from Jesus's thorn-pierced brow, but I had no inkling that act was for humanity's recovery from our separation from our Maker.

What appealed most about Jesus was his consistent pursuit of me. He knew me before I was born, and hadn't left since. At least that's what Michelle and Gretchen said. And I was learning love is a choice. My mother's choices were a contrast to my father's, and Jesus's love and death were all wrapped up in choice. It was a relief to know I at least had a heavenly Father who wouldn't abandon me.

The visits with my Catalan father—my "sperm donor," as my angst-filled teenage self began referring to him—were sporadic. As I look back now as a mother, our reunions remind me of that peculiar trait of childbirth: just enough time would go by between visits that I would forget how painful they could be and I would decide to try again. Unlike with childbirth, I didn't get to take a sweet package of unconditional love home with me.

About every six months I would get a letter in the mail with familiar handwriting and foreign stamps. Sometimes it would be an art book. A book about him with nothing more than a *"De tu padre"*—"From your father"—scrawled in the cover with the same distinct handwriting from the envelope.

The phone calls were even less frequent. My initial "Hello?" was always followed with a pause long enough to indicate the thousands of miles our voices were required to travel to reach each other. My heart stopped whenever I'd hear a long pause after I answered. On the rare occasion it was actually him and not a nervous boy calling, he would start the conversation with a proclamation: "Alexandra. It is your father." That statement, said with such confidence, became more irritating every year. I knew what a father was supposed to do. Calling once a year was not it.

Every couple of years he would offer to pay for the pricey plane ticket for me to fly over the ocean to see him. And I would go, hopeful that this would be the time that I would be captivating enough to grab hold of him and shake him out of his absence. I would return ready to receive more letters and phone calls. And I waited in silence. Jesus had to be better than what I already had.

A few weeks before Christmas of my freshman year of high school, Gretchen took me to a Christian bookstore and bought me a Bible. I walked through the bookstore like it was another museum or cultural showcase. She picked out a student Bible with added excerpts about how the stories applied to teenage life. "The Bible is divided into books. Each book has a name and is broken into chapters and verses," she explained as she flipped through pages.

Suddenly this Bible language of names and numbers I'd heard in the past had meaning. Clips of Scripture I'd heard referenced had a context. Christmas and Easter had a purpose. I'd known Santa and the Easter Bunny were make-believe for a long time. I'd just never understood that the real meaning behind the holidays had to do with God among us and the history of the world. The question now was, *Is it all for real?*

For the most part, I was on board with it. I was open to hearing that God loved me. That Jesus loved me. Maybe because I had one parent who devoted herself to me and told me how special I was, it made it easier to believe I was lovable. And it wasn't a stretch to see humanity needed a Savior. I'd seen the world; there was lots of pain. My own heart ached of things not being right. It made sense that God needed to intervene for all of our sakes.

So believing there was a God and he loved me was the easy part. But I had lots of questions about Jesus. Fully human and fully divine—how does that work? And is there really a heaven and a hell? Why are some people in and some out? What about my mom? She certainly was not talking about Jesus.

And what about all the rules? No sex before marriage? Does that mean I shouldn't have been conceived? My existence was a mistake? And there seemed to be a lot of nos related to believing in Jesus. I wanted to say I believed who he was, but did that mean I had to go along with everything else?

It's not that I had clear opinions about many of those hot-button issues, but I associated them with people I saw in downtown Seattle holding up posters that said "Repent Now." Yet based on what I was hearing from Gretchen and Michelle, Jesus was about so much more than a few rules.

Gretchen arranged her drop-offs after our Young Life meetings on Monday nights so my house on Olga Street would be her last stop. She'd turn her car ignition off, and we'd sit in the dark and dive into my questions. What is with the Trinity? If God loves us all, what's the need for Jesus? What about people in remote places of the world who have never heard of him?

But really, even with all the questions, I felt pursued by God. The idea of God, Jesus, grace—I'd never had it explained to me before, and I was drawn to it. I wanted to believe. The psalmist writes, "Should I wander off like a lost sheep—seek me! I'll recognize the sound of your voice."[1] I hadn't known I was lost until I was found; I recognized Jesus's voice calling me.

At the core of all my anxiety, all those questions, was my mom. By accepting these ideas, by accepting Jesus, was I rejecting her? The woman who gave me everything. I often couldn't see where she ended and I began. I think she was grateful for the pizza parties and movie nights that these Christian ladies invited me to be part of; they offered adult supervision and sober drivers. She didn't have to worry about the activity or who was behind the wheel, and they gave her, a single mom, a few nights off a week. But what did she think about all of this God talk I came home with? When I asked her, she simply answered, "It's not for me." No more discussion, and I was worried about what that meant for her. For us. She was not just my mother; she was my nuclear family in its totality. She was half of me. I was half of her. That kind of bond makes for difficult separation.

Back in the cabin I asked questions like, "What about all those things? All those rules? Those judgments?" not realizing that for centuries theologians had been struggling with all these same questions. That many of the smartest people in history researched and pondered and debated issues of faith without conclusive answers.

"Pray that God will fill in the gaps," Michelle said. An uncommonly open answer for a woman who tended toward black and white. "Faith is believing when you still have questions."

So I started praying. I prayed God would make clear what I needed to know and I'd be okay with the unanswered questions that were left.

Many people can point to a place and time where they said, "Yes, Lord, I know I need you, I was created to be in a relationship with you. I'm not cutting it on my own." I don't have that definite point in time. I might have believed he was who he said he was, but the list of don'ts that appeared so judgmental stopped me from crossing the line. It took two years of wrestling those doubts before I stopped fighting and prayed, "Jesus, I believe in you more than I don't believe."

ii

Boys

Accepting that the world and the people in it needed God was not difficult. Rejection and abandonment were real. It was the idea of absolute truth that was new. One truth. One God. One Savior. It went smack up against the messages of "what's right for one person may not be right for another" that I'd grown up with. And the rules for living that seemed to go with the Christian faith were confusing. They felt constraining. At the same time, they felt safe. They offered some boundaries that simplified life. It made sense that if you reduced the complication, you reduced the potential for more pain and confusion.

The emphasis my Young Life leaders placed on marriage was part of this new framework. It was a new twist on romance. On commitment. I couldn't remember my mother once mentioning marriage as something to hope for. In fact, she had a small placard propped up in our kitchen window that read, "Don't wait for your knight in shining armor; you might get left cleaning up after the horse." A cartoon of a woman dressed in a medieval peasant's dress, standing behind a horse with her shovel ready, stood under the words. I knew my mom had placed it there for both our sakes.

Despite that placard and my mother's efforts to minimize the importance of a man, I had an increased awareness of wanting something that a boy could give. I wanted to be loved. And boys offered affection, at least. Despite my tendency to be overly serious, I was a pretty girl, so I didn't have a hard time getting boys' attention. But I was also a rule follower, so many quickly lost interest when they realized I wasn't going to be part of the fun that teenage boys hope for.

Boys were a mystery to me. After my grandfather died when I was six, my entire extended family was girls. Me, my mom, her sister, and her daughter, my only cousin. I wanted to figure boys out, and flirting drew them in. Too many times I played with boys' emotions as I worked to get their interest. Today I'm grateful I don't have sons so I don't have to watch them be tortured by girls like me. I wasn't malicious or even intentional; I was just too wrapped up in my own need for affection to think about what my flirting might do to the boys around me. I wanted to know if I could capture their attentions. And once I did, the challenge was over and I moved on. I wanted male love—and I wanted some control.

The few couples I knew with long marriages—parents of friends from school—didn't appear unhappy, and yet there was something about marriage that made my mother answer the same way she did about God: "It's not for me."

In 1980, *Newsweek* magazine published a cover article that said college-educated women in their forties who had never been married were more likely to be killed by terrorists than to marry. My mother frequently talked about that with her sister and her friends. Usually with a joking tone, but as a way to say, "My chances are over."

One day, standing in our kitchen, I asked her, "Do you think there's one right person for everyone?"

"No." The answer I was expecting, but not hoping for. "There are lots of possibilities; you just have to make one work," she continued.

"But what about you? Do you think there's one right person for *you*?"

She chuckled and looked at me like she appreciated my naïveté. "Not according to *Newsweek*."

"But maybe you just haven't found each other yet."

I didn't want her to give up on love, because I still wanted a chance at it. The romance of one person committing himself to me forever was too enticing. At fifteen, I wasn't ready to give up. I wasn't ready to pick up the shovel and stand behind the horse. I still wanted to dream of the happily ever after, even if it was naïve. I didn't really think through what that would look like on a practical level once I was swept off my feet. That the happily ever after might be more centered on dishes and diapers than I realized. I wanted to focus on the romance.

Soon after that conversation, a man named Larry came on a rainy Friday night to pick my mother up for a blind date. A counselor from my mother's school had set them up. He ducked to fit through the doorway of our 1920s bungalow, and as I looked up at him, I thought of a tall evergreen tree. His trench coat accentuated his height and was dark on the shoulders where the rain had grazed him. He was a recent widower looking for companionship, and none of us knew as we shook hands that he'd come to prove *Newsweek* wrong.

A year later, my mother walked into my bedroom, where the violets on my wallpaper climbed from the hardwood floors to the ceiling. My comforter with its matching violet pattern was pulled up to my chin while I shivered underneath. The nighttime drafts in our house were a combination of old windows and our frugal lifestyle. The lace trim on my comforter was a better match for the twelve-year-old who had picked it out. I was now sixteen and felt like the room could use a makeover.

She tried to wriggle as much of her body as she could next to mine on my twin-sized bed as the tears welled up in her eyes. She and I were both surprised that Larry proposed that night. It had been a typical evening for us, a three-person date. We were in the lobby of the Edgewater Hotel on Seattle's waterfront. They were sitting on a sofa close to the fireplace, drinking their cocktails from the hotel bar. I sat a few sofas away, trying to stay up on my English homework.

I looked over my book and saw him down on one knee. I quickly lifted the book back up to cover my face. *What is he thinking? Here? Now?* I peered back over the top of my book. They were both turned, looking at me. The book went up again. I didn't want to have to respond to what I knew was happening. I didn't want a heavy conversation. I just wanted the night to go on like I expected, with hot chocolate, some pleasant ambiance, in a stylish hotel lobby.

"Things are going to change now," she said as she snuggled up to me.

I nodded. I was afraid if I tried to speak, my tears would start. I was happy for the change so she wouldn't be alone, but I knew our special twosome would never be the same. It was a bittersweet good-bye to our exclusive era, a girls' life of adventure. At the same time, it was what I wanted. I knew more love would come out of it.

"Are you okay with this?" she asked.

I nodded again, my vision blurring as the tears filled my eyes. I looked down at the field of violets covering me. And really, I was okay with it. The fact that Larry wanted to marry her was proof of how good he was. He wanted to do the right thing. And I liked him. He took us out to dinner and always included me in conversation. I didn't feel like he was just putting up with me.

And I agreed, things would change. Even though he'd been with us almost every evening the last few months, he still went home every night to his own house. We hadn't lived with a man since the one I'd called Daddy left more than ten years earlier.

"We've had a great time together."

I nodded again. I didn't say anything because I was afraid my crying would intensify, and I didn't want her to think I didn't like the idea of her getting married. I just knew I was saying good-bye to the "us" of the past. I left my chin down on my chest so my tears could move down my cheeks more easily.

I was looking for evidence of good men in the world. Of committed men who wouldn't leave. Who wouldn't leave me. He wanted to do it right. How could I not be okay with that? Besides, I was looking at colleges, getting ready to leave home, and now she wouldn't be alone. She and I both knew change was ahead anyway. I was ready to move out of the violet-lined room.

They married that summer as I got ready for my senior year of high school.

iii

Perfection

Spring came, and like any senior about to graduate, I was excited and terrified. It felt as though middle and high school were all aimed at preparing for what was next: college. All those years working to have a "well-rounded" application, getting into the right schools, and ultimately earning scholarships so I could afford to go. I researched schools, toured them, and narrowed them down to five possibilities. My applications were all in. I was now waiting for my fate through acceptance letters and financial aid packages.

I earned my first 4.0 grade point average my first semester of high school. The affirmation was addictive, and I determined to graduate with no less. Academic perfection seemed like a worthy goal. And I rounded out my college application with class president, cheerleader, and city orchestra. I added tennis team to the résumé, even though I hated going to practice and competing. I probably hated tennis because I was terrible and didn't do things I couldn't master. But I needed a sport in order to waive my PE requirements, allowing me to not jeopardize my flawless grade point average with a gym class.

Striving for the perfect college application offered a road map for what to do during my teenage years. What classes to take, after-school activities to participate in, friends to have. If this was the formula for excellence, I was going to follow it and master it. I was going to will myself to be the best. If that meant starting my weekend homework on Friday night, staying up until midnight, and studying during my lunch hour, I would. It could earn me that scholarship, that ticket to the next place, but more, it could justify that I was indeed worth noticing.

Fifteen years later, I sat in my MOPS (Mothers of Preschoolers) group in Denver, listening to a speaker talk about healthy sexual development in kids. I was nervous about the presentation because as the group's coordinator, I'd arranged for the speaker, and I wasn't sure if she would address that controversial list of rules for right living and offend the women who were my friends. Would the topic even feel relevant, considering how young our kids were? I mean, really, how much was there to say about preschoolers and sexual development? But Mary came highly recommended and was free, so I booked her.

I could tell right away she was connecting with the group. She covered sexual abuse, how to talk to three-year-olds about their bodies, and appropriate touch. She told stories of her own abuse and how it impacted her marriage.

My friend Jen raised her hand and asked, "What about being naked in front of your kids?"

"I never saw my parents naked, and my kids see me get in and out of the shower."

I sat in the front row, pleased as moms interrupted Mary with their questions. They weren't offended; they couldn't get enough. She was talking about the influence of same-sex and opposite-sex parents on their kids, and how the absence of one parent could impact a child's development. Then Mary said something that felt like a bullhorn in my face.

"If a girl's father is absent"—the hairs on the back of my neck started to stand in anticipation of what she was about to say—"she tends to fall into one of two categories. She becomes either sexually promiscuous, trying to get men's attention and affection, or a perfectionist, trying to prove she is worthy of love."

There it was—*clunk*. The mirror had been lifted and the reflection was clear: a perfectionist trying to prove she was worthy of love. In an instant, memories of academic anxiety, of falling short in the tangible measuring sticks of high school life, came flooding to mind. I had a new clarity about what pushed my teenage self to be so good at everything all the time.

The spring of my senior year of high school, I attended a Christian leadership conference for students in Olympia, the state's capital. The overhead lighting was stark, and even though there were no windows, I knew it was raining outside. I was clearly one of the youngest in the conference's hotel ballroom. I sat in my chair holding my notebook and pen, waiting. I opened the notebook. Closed it. Opened it again and hoped I looked busy. The other students played similar games, opening their Bibles and pretending to read, shuffling through their bags, looking for something, anything, as long as it looked like they were comfortable sitting alone.

The conference speaker was introduced as an NFL player. Though I'd never watched an entire professional football game, his name sounded familiar. As he climbed the steps to the stage, his broad frame and chiseled jaw confirmed his career. He quickly started into his story of coming to faith, but what stood out to me was his story of finding love, tangible love, in his wife. They met in college. He was a bad boy, and she convinced him to be different. They saved themselves for marriage so they could prove their self-control to each other. A commitment to show they weren't in it for the immediate gratification but for a lifetime relationship.

I could feel my heart melting into a buttery mess on the hotel carpet underneath me. To have someone that strong say, "I will wait for you, I will take care of you"—that's what I wanted. I knew it went against the "you don't need a man to be happy" principle my mother worked so hard to instill. But I wanted it anyway.

I mastered the high school formula for success; it was pretty clear I was going to make it to graduation with my 4.0 intact and a valedictorian title. By my schooling standards, I measured up at perfect. But my heartache persisted. Maybe what I needed was a formula for love. And God felt too distant, too intangible. The key must be finding the right man. One who chose to live by the rules and to stick it out. Someone who proved trustworthy on the front end so there wouldn't be risk of regret later. The result would be someone—a man, a husband—who would not leave. Who instead would wrap his arms around me, protect me, and never let go.

iv

Choose Me

Three years later, I sat down on the cold linoleum of my sorority house floor clutching the pile of mail that had built up while I'd been home over Christmas vacation. I wanted to turn inward, to shut out the seventy other sorority girls sitting on the floor around me, gathering for another planning meeting on recruiting freshmen into our fold. Their collective chatter was an ocean of noise that was familiar and suddenly annoying. There was one envelope I was anxious to open, the one with the international stamps and familiar handwriting. It had been months since I'd heard from my dad, and I wondered why my heart rate quickened just knowing the letter existed.

The meeting was called to order, and I was able to ignore the chipper announcements and rally cry from the front to focus on the letter. Tearing open the envelope, I saw more of the familiar handwriting. As I read, I wondered why he chose to use Spanish this time. Had I told him I was a Spanish major? My studies made it easy to decipher the language; it was his handwriting that was difficult to make out.

Like usual, I read through quickly, hoping there would be something monumental, an apology, a promise that a check for tuition was on its way, an admission of some kind that he had failed me. The second read was always a disappointed combing through for details that would at least hint at the possibility of the monumentals that I didn't catch the first time around. But this time I got stuck halfway through the first read. For a moment I felt the air stop moving in and out of my lungs. The blinking began, trying to stop the tears from happening in this room full of pep and cheer.

"A baby," the letter read. A baby girl, in fact. He'd had another baby.

How could he? How old was he? Who was this woman, the mother? How old was *she*? I started looking around the room for an exit plan; the tears couldn't be held off much longer. Stepping over the six girls between me and the door would draw more attention than staying where I was and wiping my wet face with my sweatshirt sleeve. I let the tears eke out slowly so my wiping could keep up with them.

I kept reading, looking at each word, making sure I understood every possible meaning. There was no mistaking—he'd had another daughter and he wanted me to come to Barcelona to meet her. How could he so blatantly fail to take care of me and think it would be a good idea to father another child? Was it possible to feel jealousy and pity for someone at the same time? Was it possible to be angry at a baby for taking what I thought should be mine? Obviously it was. And he wanted me to visit? So I could see what I was missing?

Though it sounded like torture, I knew I had to go. This baby could be my link. I pictured her as a teenager coming to visit me, her American big sister. I'd be married, with kids of my own. She would probably smoke since she was European, and I would make her smoke out on the back patio. I'd be cool enough to allow the smoking but responsible enough to keep it away from the kids. This could be my shot at a connection to the half of me that was still absent.

"And where are you staying?" the lady behind the Plexiglas asked me without looking up from my passport.

"With my father." The words *my father* sounded less strange because the conversation was in Spanish. Everything in Spanish already felt forced.

"His address?" Again without looking up.

"I'm not sure."

"We need an address."

I felt the eyes of the people behind me in line, glaring as I scrambled through my backpack looking for something that might have his address. I was a minute and an escalator away from seeing my father, my heart already pounding. *She probably thinks I should know my father's address. She thinks I'm lying, that I'm trying to sneak into Europe to hop trains for the next six months. Do I look like every other American college student planning to hang out in Europe for the next year? Filling up the subway stations, sleeping on my backpack? Can't she tell I'm different? That I belong here?*

"He lives here. In Barcelona." Did I have an address book? I must have brought something. Shuffling through the textbooks I didn't read on the plane, I thought, *I'm already behind on schoolwork.* What was I thinking when I packed them? This was my spring break, after all.

"Fine," she finally said, peering over the tops of her reading glasses. "Go ahead." She motioned her hand toward the top of the escalator.

As I rode the escalator down to the baggage terminal, the light from the three-story windows poured into the airport. I saw him at the foot of the escalator, standing alone, looking up, smiling. I wanted to run. Run away and run to him. At the bottom of the escalator, he approached me and put his arms around me. I pulled away and leaned in at the same time, resulting in an awkward hug. He lifted his hand and stroked his finger on my face. I felt rage fly up from inside my chest to my extremities. I wanted to shout, "You have no right to do that! To touch me that way!" But instead I held it in and avoided eye contact. Why was this always so hard?

Since he didn't drive, we took a cab back to his apartment, where the baby and her mother were waiting. We walked past the doorman, and I wondered if he knew who I was. We stepped into the caged elevator to go up to his apartment. I looked at my father standing next to me. He looked older than ever now, his hair whiter and thinner than at our last visit, more age spots on his face and neck. What business did he have fathering a child?

I was curious about this woman. How could she find this old man attractive? But I wanted to be kind. To both the baby and her mother. It wasn't their fault my father had ignored me, disappointed me in so many ways for so many years. I pitied them that they were at the beginning of this journey. I was afraid I might know how their script would play out. Despite my jealousy, for their sakes I hoped it would be different.

We walked through the apartment door, and a dark-haired woman, probably in her thirties, stood facing us. She held a baby against her chest. Her dark eyes moved quickly from me to my father and back to me. I kept walking toward her. I knew I needed to take control of the awkwardness and show her I was willing to be the first one to reach out. I smiled, and her shoulders relaxed. I put my finger out for the baby to grasp.

Once introductions were made, it was hard to take the conversation anywhere else. Should I follow up with, "So how did you two meet?" There was no natural lead-in to getting to know each other. My Spanish was better than it had ever been, but her native language was French. It was easier to focus on the baby, so I moved my finger up and down, and the baby's tiny fingers wrapped around mine and moved with it. The baby put my finger in her mouth, and her mother and I both laughed. Making eye contact, we smiled and understood neither one of us wanted to be angry with the other. We had a strange set of circumstances connecting us, but there was no hostility.

After lunch, my father and I went down the caged elevator to his studio. Despite the years apart and my entire childhood to catch up on, we had nothing to say. Finally he motioned to the ceiling and his new family a few stories above us.

"She wanted to have a baby."

As if that explained everything. The years of absence. The months with no contact. Fathering another daughter when he continued to fail me. I felt the anger in my fingertips.

"Your mom. She wanted a baby too," he continued.

I knew that was a lie. My mother loved me, but she'd always made it clear I was a surprise. But I didn't care if a smidge of what he said was true. Did he know she had a scar on the back of her right thigh from trying to protect me? Did he know that twenty years earlier she was carrying me in her arms down a Barcelona street and tripped, and as she felt herself falling face forward toward the fence and the glass bank window it protected, her mothering instincts took over, and she swiveled her body and sat on the wrought-iron spoke, stabbing a hole in her leg? Did he know that a man—certainly not him, but a stranger—was passing by in a cab and stopped and took her to the hospital to be cared for? In her adrenaline rush, she was so concerned that I was okay she didn't even realize she had punctured herself.

Or how about the everyday, the getting up, the taking me to school, the doctor's appointments, the recitals, the parent-teacher conferences? Taking on a second job so she could pay for my flute when I was in middle school, and again to pay for caps on my teeth when I was in high school? My life was filled with millions of opportunities to tangibly love me, and my mother showed up. She chose me above everything.

Did he know *that's* what a parent does? That's the kind of choice a parent makes? That's what love looks like?

Section 3

Trust

i

TRAJECTORY

I walked into our off-campus house and threw my backpack on the orange velour sofa. Keeping my raincoat on, I continued into the kitchen, wondering if there was anything in the fridge I could mooch off my roommates without them noticing. As I passed by the house phone, I glanced up at the whiteboard above it on the off chance there was a message for me. "ALEX, your husband called!!!" was written in red dry-erase marker. I knew just who the message was referring to, and my heart rate quickened.

"You should look at the Dale House," my friend Corynn said in our sorority house living room a few months earlier. Corynn had graduated the year before and was back visiting campus. She stopped at the sorority house during our weekly chapter meeting, knowing she'd catch lots of people at once to say hi. We snuck out of the meeting to talk about the stress surrounding my impending graduation and my total lack of plans despite my search for something meaningful. Though much of my faith talk through college still focused on the outward, the dos and don'ts, I was growing bit by bit in the understanding of a deeper calling.

Corynn's description of the Dale House, a group home for troubled teenagers in Colorado Springs, was intriguing. It seemed to put Christian faith in action in a way that was different from short-term service trips I'd taken in college, which did good work but gave no credit to the source of love. At the same time, I was skeptical of missions trips that focused on growing people's faith though they lacked basic needs. What I heard was a description of a place where action and faith were inseparable. I wanted to hear more.

"And Derek Kuykendall is there. Do you remember him?"

"Oh. . . . Yeah." Conscious of my facial expression, I tried to look as nonchalant as possible.

"He went right after graduation and stayed."

Derek Kuykendall. I'd watched him from a distance. There was a small, tight Christian community on campus, and though we were both part of that group and attended the same weekly gatherings for our two years of overlap, we'd only spoken a few times. He had always made me swoon a little, because unlike many of the other guys in the group, he was soft-spoken, not drawing attention to himself. In his quiet confidence he stood out. There was no question I knew who he was.

Despite the distraction of hearing Derek's name, I was drawn in by Corynn's description of the Dale House as she talked about living with kids who were aging out of the foster care or juvenile corrections systems. Graduation was only a couple of months away, and panic about the rest of my life was setting in. There is something just a tad stressful about having the option to do "anything you want." I was feeling the burden of choice and opportunity.

My Spanish/International Affairs major pointed me in the direction of living overseas after graduation like my mom did. But my semester studying in Mexico the year before was lonely, and I didn't feel I needed the globe-trotting adventures my classmates were planning. They wanted to explore the world they'd learned about the last four years. I'd spent my childhood exploring that world, and I wanted the opposite: some stability. And I wanted to start this grown-up life on a certain trajectory, trusting God to take me to unexpected places. But mostly I was panicking and looking for something to do, somewhere to go.

I packed my bags with my cutest grunge-inspired slacker clothes and flew to Colorado Springs to stay for a weekend, to see and hear and feel the community. When I got off the airplane, Derek was waiting at my gate. Even though I'd known his friends and where he sat in our campus cafeteria years earlier, I'd never spoken more than three sentences to him. As we walked to the baggage claim, I tried to sound interesting and profound, again in a nonchalant kind of way.

The staff was consumed with running a household of thirty, so I spent the next three days following them around as they did their work: cooking dinner for the masses, mopping the floors, arguing with a kid about curfew, and driving another kid to Walmart. This group of mostly twentysomething recent college graduates was actively caring for kids who'd never lived in a stable home. And though many of the "adults" were just above legal age themselves, they took on the responsibility of reframing the world for these teenagers. Showing them that some people did follow through with what they said, forgave when teenagers made teenager mistakes, offered consequences that fit the offense with emotions that were tempered and without their fists.

Sitting on the airplane on the way home, I watched out the window as my bags were loaded into the cargo portion below. As I started to pray, asking God to show me if I was meant to come back, I knew I already had the answer. I felt God impressing it on my heart: I would come back. And for more than one purpose: to be at the Dale House *and* to be with Derek.

There is only a smattering of times I've felt God's clear direction. This was the first of those experiences.

Tears rolled down my cheeks, and I was overwhelmed at the thought of having direction from the Artist who had formed the Rocky Mountains in the distance. There is a difference between saying God knows me and believing it. And an even greater difference between believing it and having evidence of it.

As the tears flowed, I absorbed God's provision through the details of the Dale House. Of being sent to a place that seemed to so perfectly fit who I was and what I was looking for. The staff trusted that their actions spoke of God's love with more clarity than any words. Where extending grace came first, and changed behavior was expected only after kids knew they were in a place where they were safely loved. And the possibility of a man who was pulled in the same direction, to the same place, for more than just service—for me. I'd found the starting place for my grown-up life trajectory.

A month later, looking up at the whiteboard in my college house kitchen, I laughed at my roommates' nickname for Derek. I could feel my heart rate rise at even knowing he'd thought about me. He'd probably called for some clarification on my application, but I could hope there was something more. A reason it was him who called rather than someone else. That he was as expectant as I was about what the next year held.

ii

Impressions

Mortified would be a light term for how I felt. But I was so thankful to be done riding the bike, out of the freezing air, and back in the van. The day before, the Dale House staff piled into the group home vans with bikes and bags of extra clothes for a two-day orientation of sorts, which included a bike ride over Vail Pass. As in riding over the Continental Divide, the mountain range that separates our country's east from west.

My sea-level Seattle lungs and discount mountain bike did not prepare me for this group bonding activity. I'd arrived in Colorado only two weeks earlier. I was relieved on the first day of the bike excursion when a rare September snowstorm hit and the riding was optional. What totally baffled me were the others in the group who opted to ride in the blowing snow.

I'd already suspected I might not fit in with the rugged culture of the place. Though the Pacific Northwest was similar to Colorado in its affinity for the outdoor lifestyle, my idea of getting outside was hitting the sales at an open-air mall.

Soon after I arrived, I was sitting in the staff meeting room with my Bible, waiting for others to meander in for our group Bible study. George, the director, walked by in his wire-frame glasses and his black motorcycle jacket hanging over his marathon-running skeleton frame, a box of cigarettes tucked in his front chest pocket. He looked down at the table and laughed.

"A pink Bible?!" he shouted. "Ha, I've never seen a pink Bible before!"

I looked down at the pink leather cover of my Bible with my name embossed in silver letters across the front. I felt my shoulders drop as I tried to slink down in my chair. No one had ever commented on the color of my Bible before. I was suddenly aware I was wearing mascara.

It stopped snowing overnight, and the second day's ride was not optional. As soon as I started pedaling, I knew I was in trouble. The air going in my lungs seemed to be decreasing with each breath. I'd like to say it was altitude sickness—I was too newly arrived from sea level—but really I was out of shape with a terrible bike and no gloves, riding in the biting cold. I quickly fell behind the rest of the group, and the pity riders started showing up—guys who had no problem riding extra by doubling back to ride with me and bring up the rear.

"How you doing?" one asked as he pulled up next to me and slowed down to match my sluggish pace. I could tell the lilt in his voice was forced, like being friendly would somehow make up for my lack of athleticism.

I could feel myself getting more annoyed with every push of my foot. What was up with everyone else? With all these other girls? Did I miss the fitness test when I was out for my interview?

The gap between me and the next person ahead continued to grow until I could no longer see her. I felt vomit rising in my throat. I tried to swallow and hold it back—I didn't want to throw up in front of the pity rider of the moment—but I finally had to stop my bike, lean over, and let it out. It became clear the only way I was going to go over Vail Pass was in a motorized vehicle.

"Alex needs to stop."

"She can't go any farther."

"Derek, can you drive her to the end?"

I heard these statements floating above my head as if they were about somebody else. So relieved the torture ride was ending, I still wanted to shrink into oblivion with each declaration. And now I was going to be alone with Derek in the van? Looking like this? With no makeup, clothes that weren't flattering, and dark circles under my eyes? Failing at any attempt to be outdoorsy and cool? So pathetic? Really?

And then once we were in the van, he had to be nice about it, to try to make me feel better. "I wanted an excuse to stop riding," he said.

Still shivering, I thought I might disintegrate from embarrassment. I looked straight ahead out the windshield and tried to think of something witty to say. Nothing came to mind.

My discomfort was heightened by what had happened the night before. The staff sat in a large circle around the living room of the house where we were staying, going around and one by one answering a question to get to know each other. Many of us had arrived in the last month, and though I'd only been there a few weeks, after spending every minute with the staff in such an intense environment, I felt like we were building rapport quickly. But not so quickly that I was ready to share my biggest hurts with everyone at once.

It was my turn to answer the question, and within the first minute I felt my voice cracking. Within two minutes I couldn't talk; the crying was getting in the way. I don't remember what the question was or even my answer, really. I remember the ugly, snotty, messy sobbing that forced others to scramble to find me tissues and lean in to listen with concerned expressions. And that it was about my dad. I remember I was embarrassed by this sudden and unplanned show of vulnerability. It came on so quickly, which meant it was close to the surface. And there was so much snot. How was I supposed to clean it up with everyone looking at me?

I didn't want to talk about my dad. I hated talking about him. And I was afraid the way it came out would make me look out of control, too broken myself, too vulnerable to help the kids we were there to help. And it was the only show of emotion of that level that night. It felt too exposed and too intense for what the sharing time was supposed to look like. I couldn't talk and motioned with my hand to move on to the next person. I hoped she was as messed up as I was. I was disappointed to hear she wasn't.

After everyone shared and the circle broke up, a few people approached me to ask if I was okay. I wanted to scream, "Of course I'm not okay. I'm a mess!" but I'd already made a scene. All of the years of holding it in, and it came out right here with an audience of fifteen. I wanted a chance to do it over, to come off presentable, collected.

Derek came up to me and tried to be nice. He remembers saying, "I had no idea. About your dad." All I remember was thinking he was thoughtful and hoping I would become camouflaged by the sofa I was sitting on.

So, doubly embarrassed, I sat in the passenger seat of the van and tried to think how I could redeem my image in front of this very cool guy. I was thankful to have one-on-one time with him, but I could think of about a thousand different ways I would have liked it to come about. Ways that involved him initiating rather than responding to my crisis.

Ever since that football player in Olympia spoke, I'd had an image of a man who would love and take care of me. A man who was stable and kind and principled. All through college I'd prayed for God to send me someone to protect me. Someone to start a family with, to share in my new beginning. I knew Derek had that potential, but I didn't want him to see these needy parts that were already seeping out, spilling in front of him in a big mess. I was still trying hard to hold it in.

iii

SECRETS

Lisa and I sat in the parked car, putting off reentering the chaos of life in the community, or "on the block," the term we used to describe the cluster of homes that made up the Dale House Project. We'd been away for an hour—a trip to get a soda and a temporary reprieve for her from her identity as a group home kid.

Lisa sat next to me not moving, and I sensed she wanted me to keep pushing the conversation. She held her large cup of soda in her hand, and I could hear the ice clink as she shifted her weight in the passenger's seat. We'd had similar conversations before, and she'd blown off my questions with a sarcastic "Wouldn't you like to know?"

I wanted her to believe she was worth pursuing, so I repeated my words: "You can tell me what happened."

Lisa looked at me out of the side of her eyes, smirking. She knew she held power in that moment, a rare feeling for her.

I wanted us to be close, to be her big sister figure, for her to like me. In some ways I was like a five-foot-two, 110-pound, white-girl puppy running circles around her, wanting her approval. She was offering me perspective on my own disappointments; her life was helping me better understand mine. She was finishing her sentence with the courts for assault, and her anger spewed everywhere—in her spiteful comments, her physical posturing, telling anyone who would listen she would hurt them before they had a chance to hurt her. I knew this kind of overflowing anger had a story behind it. I suspected I knew what it was in general terms, but I wanted her to trust me with the details.

Lisa shifted her weight again. Her body carried many extra pounds, she may have weighed almost double what I did, and her dark brown face was covered in acne. She smelled of a combination of ripe body odor and cigarette smoke. Her hair fell out of its ponytail around her face like a halo of frizzy curls. I suspected her poor self-care was evidence of past sexual abuse, her way of guaranteeing no one would be attracted to her like that again. But she hadn't confirmed my suspicions. Yet.

"You can trust me," I said.

Her smirk didn't go away. I knew those words sounded cheap. Trust? What was that to a seventeen-year-old girl who'd been abandoned by the world? Who tried to hide in a body of fat and stench to protect herself? Who looked at me with my size 2 jeans and seemingly perfect life? How could she ever trust me? But I had been working for months at being consistent with her. Making small promises and following through. Taking her on trips, like this one to get a soda, to listen for the feelings behind her words and affirm them. Driving her to her GED tests and picking her up with an excited "How'd it go?" Doing my twenty-two-year-old best to fill in as many gaps as I could from her years of holes. I was practicing giving those important parenting messages: "You are valuable. You are precious."

"My brother touched me," she said. She looked at me out of the corner of her eyes again to assess my reaction.

Very aware of my face, I nodded to show her I wasn't going to be shocked. That she didn't need to be ashamed. "I'm sorry."

Knowing there were no words that would take away the terrible that had happened in her life. That any attempt at condolences would just seem hollow and fake.

"He would come in my room and have sex with me." Again she looked out of the side of her eyes.

Again I nodded, prompting her to keep talking. I willed my face to show her she wasn't at fault. She didn't have to hide the truth.

"I'm sorry," I said again. Although I could feel my body tensing up, I wanted to protect her from my reactions. I didn't want her to know my stomach was turning at the thought of someone climbing in bed with her and using her. So, for her sake, I kept nodding.

Then the shock waves started.

"He got me pregnant."

We had now surpassed any grotesque details I could have come up with on my own. I knew she didn't have a baby. She answered my unspoken question just as it was starting to float through my mind.

"My parents made me have an abortion." Her voice started wavering. I could sense her barricade of anger was beginning to fragment. She kept talking, further widening the crevice of self-protection.

"They didn't believe me." She started crying. "My brother denied it and they didn't believe me." Her shoulders fell, and she laid her chin on her chest and let the tears roll down her acne-covered cheeks. I knew she didn't like being touched—I now knew much better why—so I reached out my arm closest to her and put it around her shoulder as a test to see if she would accept a hug. She leaned back into the crook of my arm, rested her head on my shoulder, and I wrapped her in an embrace. The ice in her cup clinked as her body shook. I was grateful she didn't ask where God was when all of this happened, because I didn't have an answer.

"They didn't believe me" were the words laced with the most pain.

"I believe you," I said. "You can trust me."

After a few minutes of muffled sobs, her body relaxed. She kept her head on my shoulder. Her hair was in my face, and I smelled the cigarette smoke. I wondered when she'd last washed it. I wasn't going to let this moment go, this moment of trust I'd been working toward. I let her decide when it was time to get out of the car.

The next day I stood in the kitchen of the main house, loading the industrial dishwasher and thinking through my next steps with Lisa. As I scraped pieces of egg off the plates into the trash barrel on wheels, I wondered what she needed from me.

Breakfast for twenty was done, and kids were leaving for school and jobs. A few waited outside, smoking, to meet with the onsite teacher to prepare for upcoming GED exams. Trying to get twenty teenagers off the couch and out the door for the day was like plowing through marshmallow paste.

I closed the dishwasher door and looked out the window at two boys playing basketball in the single-hoop driveway court, passing time until their tutoring appointments. Their short, brown bodies were far from NBA height, but they were used to puffing them up to make themselves appear as big as possible. They had on almost identical outfits: form-fitting white tank tops and black Dickies that barely rested on their hips. They waved their arms in the air with choppy up-and-down motions, a sloppy street sort of basketball. Sixteen and seventeen years old, the hair on their upper lips suggesting they were doing everything possible to muster up mustaches. And then the younger one started laughing. His head tipped back and his smile pointed to the sky. Despite his teenage attempts at facial hair, I saw a flash of the little boy that was still in him. A quick glimpse of the children hidden in these rough boys who'd already started lives of crime.

Instantly I was struck by the sacredness of that place. A place that allowed two young men to play a kids' game. Straddling childhood and manhood, they were offered a chance to place both feet on the childhood side for a moment, to capture, for just a few minutes, something ripped from them.

I grabbed the countertop as emotion took over. I stood frozen as the tears came rushing out and gratitude and grief rushed over me. Gratitude for a place that resembled heaven on earth, where Lisa and these boys who'd never had a safe home to go back to now did. Gratitude that God was allowing me to be part of it. And grief for the broken state of the world, more dark and painful than I'd realized. Grief for the kids at the Dale House. And for me. And gratitude once more: that God pursued us all. Pursued me. And offered me hope in my hurting places.

iv

SURRENDER

Over time, Derek's attention seemed to be gravitating my way. Now as I look back, his interest was obvious. But then, I was so nervous about getting my hopes up only to have them later squelched, I questioned every invitation and the motives behind them. I wanted to believe they were indicators that he was interested, but my fear took over and told me to protect my heart and not get excited. He asked me to go out for dinner after work, to go to coffee on our day off, to pick him up from the airport when he came home from a weekend of visiting mutual college friends. It's obvious now, but my insecurities, my fear of eventual abandonment, told me then to protect.

Finally I got it. He was more forthright, and I was ready to hear. We were both in wonder that our lives were connecting. It was wonderful, full of wonder, that this handsome, strong, sensitive, Jesus-pursuing man would be taken with me in the same way I was with him. There was an understanding that this wasn't a casual relationship, a "let's just date and see what happens." We were sure if this "worked," it was for a lifetime.

And though it felt wonderful, it also felt terrifying. I didn't want to do anything that would prompt him to leave. So I avoided tension. He decided on our dates, what we did, where we ate, how we progressed. I'm not really sure why he continued pursuing me. I was generally silent and wide-eyed, a pretty boring girlfriend. He now says it forced him to step up and initiate, but he agrees I was a mystery in many ways.

"I think we should do pre-engagement counseling," Derek told me one day.

My heart stopped. What did that mean? Was engagement the direction he thought we were going? Was the counseling going to determine whether or not he proposed? If so, it sounded like a loaded activity. Loaded with potential affirmation or disaster. I stayed silent.

"Well, I've heard of other couples doing it," he continued. "You know, once you're engaged, you've kind of decided you're getting married."

This was sounding like an even worse idea.

"Besides, our health insurance will cover six sessions. We should do it before we leave."

It was spring at the Dale House, and we had about five more months before we moved on. Not wanting to sound like I had anything to hide, I agreed. "Sure."

Before our first session, we went to the counselor's office and filled out a questionnaire.

"Sit apart, where you can't see each other's answers," the counselor instructed us. I looked at Derek. He rolled his eyes. I tried not to laugh.

We used number two pencils to fill in bubbles to questions about extended family, finances, and hopes for life. Many of the topics seemed irrelevant, things I'd never thought of before. Did I consider myself a saver or a spender? I'd never had any money to determine one way or another. The topics that weren't irrelevant seemed obvious. I knew what I wanted: a traditional family, kids, division of labor, stability.

We turned in our computer answer sheets to the counselor. "You'll get your results in two weeks when you have your first appointment," she said as she took our papers. I didn't think I could wait two weeks to find out if we were considered compatible.

The counseling sessions were rather uneventful. I went into each one hoping she would declare us a guaranteed success as a married couple. Instead she commented on how quiet I was. I did my best to answer questions with "whatever he said" without actually using those words.

At the end of our six sessions, she declared "no red flags." Then she turned to me. "There is one thing that I think *you* need to explore."

I felt the spotlight blaring down.

"I don't think you've fully worked through your father's absence."

What does that have to do with anything? I thought. *With my relationship with Derek?* Though there was a tiny part of me that knew it was true.

"I'm fine," I answered, my defenses up. I tried to catch a glimpse of Derek out of the side of my eye to gauge his reaction.

"I would recommend you get some counseling on your own to come to some resolution there."

She was calling me out, exposing me as damaged goods. Even though I'd tried to call as little attention to myself as possible during our six insurance-covered sessions, the needy, pathetic girl who was abandoned was still obvious. Who had daddy issues that any suitor should steer clear from. I was the problem getting in the way of us moving forward.

"Other than that, you seem pretty compatible on the big things."

Other than that. Other than me and all my baggage, we should be fine.

Weeks later in Derek's apartment, he wrapped his arms around me and pulled me close. I was done trying to hide, keeping my wounds covered, living every moment afraid that he would see enough and decide I was too much of a basket case to go on. I let my sobs fall into his shoulder. I cried for the girl I was who desperately wanted her daddy's attention and never got it. For the teenager who worked so hard to be perfect to prove her worth. For the scared young woman who had fallen in love and was terrified she wasn't worth sticking around for.

"Trust me," he said in a quiet voice. "I'm not going anywhere."

I tightened my grip around his waist and surrendered to trust.

Section 4

Legacy

i

Fights

The year that followed was filled with moving back to the Pacific Northwest, wedding plans, and conflict. We decided to move to Portland to try dating in the real world, away from the intensity of the Dale House, before getting engaged. Really, Derek came up with that plan and I went along with it. Two months of real-world dating was long enough, and the day after Thanksgiving, Derek was down on one knee asking me to share life with him until death do us part.

Though the engagement did feel like the promise I'd been waiting for, the deepest insecurities were still there. As we chose flowers and guests, the short remarks came out under the guise of fighting over wedding details. When really it was me fighting against myself, my worries, that this dream could really be coming true—a man I adored was choosing me forever.

If I were to plan my wedding again, I wouldn't have put so much energy into selecting bridesmaids' dresses and invitations. I would have used those months to face my emotional junk head-on. I would have better handled my mom's skepticism of my decision to get married young. Been more confident in the life decisions

I was making that were different from hers. Examined my fears that *husband* would be another word that could be defined as "one who abandons." Instead I held it in, was stressed on my big day, and snapped at the photographer.

No surprise our first year of marriage was difficult. The leaving and cleaving process is painful for anyone. Facing the other person with their morning breath and stench-soaked socks loses the romance about the first time it happens.

I was fortunate that I was desperately in love with Derek. It helped when the predictable fights about sex, money, and in-laws went down. I didn't question whether I'd married the right person. I just didn't understand why everything felt like a song being played out of tune.

On our first anniversary we let the phone's rings echo through our apartment until the answering machine picked up.

"Hi! You've reached Derek and Alex." I could hear my own voice, recorded months earlier, filling the room. I'd been so excited to say those words, "Derek and Alex"—now one number, one unit. "We can't come to the phone right now," my voice continued.

I glared over at Derek sitting on my college futon that acted as the apartment's central piece of furniture. I softly laughed, hoping that would break the tension. We couldn't come to the phone right now, that was for sure; we weren't in the mood to talk to anyone.

"Leave us a message," my voice practically sang to the caller on the other line. *BEEEEP!*

"Well, calling to wish you a happy anniversary." My father-in-law's voice rang through the apartment. "Since it's your paper anniversary, you're probably out spending lots of paper money."

"Ha!" I said, looking at Derek. You would think—out celebrating our first year of marital bliss! But no, we were fighting. Fighting about my disappointment with his anniversary gift: a wooden drying rack for the dishes. Fighting about the fact that he hadn't made plans for us to go out that night because he assumed eating out the previous Saturday night counted as our celebration. Fighting about my generally critical attitude.

"Is this a joke?" I'd asked as I unwrapped the gift. I was almost speechless, but able to muster up that question.

"I thought you'd like it. I bought it at that kitchen store at Lloyd Center. You'll use it every day," he continued. His motives were probably thoughtful—splurging on something from a foodie store I liked but couldn't afford to shop at—but his conclusions were dead wrong.

"You think *I'll* use it every day? How about *you* using it every day?"

"Why do you always assume the worst of me? I thought you'd like it."

It was the kind of fight where the drying rack started to represent his attitude about my role as the dishwasher in our relationship. And that morphed into his perception of my role as housekeeper in general. In his mind, my instant criticism of the gift characterized my general attitude about him. "You always" and "You never" started to fly around the room until we were sitting on opposite sides—him on the futon, me on the sheet-covered chair from my violet-decorated childhood bedroom—staring at each other in silence.

Our disappointments in the day were representing our disappointments in the last year. Like all newlyweds, we brought distinct expectations to the altar on our wedding day. Mine were based largely on Hallmark commercials and observations from the handful of lasting marriages I saw growing up. My senior year of high school, I'd lived in a newlywed home. My mom and Larry brought lifetimes of experiences and expectations to their relationship that offered unique challenges. So I didn't see them as a realistic model for what marriage and its arguments looked like.

There was an upside to all the fighting. It indicated I was starting to feel safe enough to disagree. Derek had married me, and I knew he intended it to be for life. So I could let my guard down a little. I could start having a voice. I think he was relieved I was starting to have opinions.

"You don't pay enough attention to me," I said when my father-in-law was done leaving his anniversary well-wishes.

Derek's face was a combination of disbelief and frustration. It silently barked, *Are you kidding me?*

I kept talking. "I don't feel it. I don't feel loved."

I was starting to get desperate. Not sure really what I wanted to say, but we were so deep into the argument I was trying to claw myself out of the hole I'd created with my earlier words. To prove that he was at fault. For the situation. For my feelings.

"What do you want from me?" He was exasperated. How could he possibly meet all of my needs?

And that's when I realized it. I really did expect him to meet all of my needs. I'd heard people say you can't expect that from your spouse; you must turn to God to meet your needs. But that all sounded like a bunch of Christian noise. Besides, I was going to have a different kind of marriage, a "you complete me" kind of marriage. In the same instant that I realized my expectations, I saw how faulty they were. Two imperfect people cannot one healed woman make. Only Jesus could do that.

As cliché as it felt, I was expecting Derek to be my Savior. Expecting him to fill the burning hole my father had left. To love me so intensely I would know my worth. When I say it now, it sounds foolishly unrealistic, but I'd lived so long thinking, *When I'm married, then . . .*

I'll feel loved.
I'll be happy.
I'll be secure.

Realizing all of this, I was angry. Angry at him and at God. I knew my expectations were the root of the conflict, but I'd been working the last hour to prove how right I was and how wrong Derek was. It was hard to suddenly flip and admit my own blaring fault in the issue. I wanted to stay mad at him. Why couldn't he be more than he was humanly intended to be? I knew it was ridiculous, but that's what I wanted.

And I was mad at God. I didn't want him to be the one I had to turn to—that sounded lonely. I wanted someone tangible. A man who would hug me and kiss me and tell me he loved me in an audible voice. Who would buy me romantic gifts that would be perfect in every way: beautiful AND practical and not over budget. For him to be perfect in every way.

Derek got up and walked down the hall to our bedroom. As he walked by, I wanted him to stop. To apologize. But he kept walking, and I sat staring at the carpet. Left to pray, "God, help me."

ii

HEROES

A few months later, Derek and I took the subway from the Paris airport to our hotel, blocks away from the Eiffel Tower. The straps from the camping backpack cut into my shoulders from the excessive weight bearing down. As we stood holding on to the subway car's poles, I looked at Derek with his equally huge backpack and felt ridiculous. The Parisians seated around us stared at us, the obvious tourists who'd overpacked, their faces blank slates. Oh why did we think we needed so much? We were playing the role of the ugly Americans with our Costco packing mentalities. My mother trained me better.

My father was living in France with my sister and her mother, a native Frenchwoman. I hadn't invited them to our wedding a year earlier in the off chance they might actually show up. There was no question I wanted Larry to walk me down the aisle, and the thought of the potential tension was enough to make me want to hide. So there was one thing I needed to happen for Derek to understand my complexities: I needed him to meet my father. And I wanted him to see the places of my childhood, Barcelona and Terni, to better understand this wide-eyed girl he'd married.

He'd never been to Europe before, and I wanted him to see, smell, hear, and feel the places that shaped me.

Plane tickets weren't cheap for a one-income couple who took the calculator to the grocery store. Derek was in the throes of full-time graduate school, and I was working for Catholic Charities, translating for migrant parents and students at a rural high school. Every penny was precious. But Derek's grandparents, Mama and Papa, gave us some money for a wedding gift. They wanted us to buy life insurance; we wanted to go on a European vacation. Derek had the summer off, so we packed our backpacks for a five-week trek.

Paris was our first stop and one of the only places on our itinerary I hadn't been. So Rick Steves's books told us where to stay and what to see in the iconic city. It was August, and Paris was deserted. Shops had metal gates pulled shut for the month. The only Parisians left seemed to be those who catered to the tourists, so we walked from site to site as if it was Disneyland and we were hitting all the major rides without the lines. We shared a baguette and cheese on the banks of the Seine, and I laughed when we kissed.

Before we took the train to see my father and his growing family, we wanted to make one small detour. To see the beaches at Normandy where Derek's grandfather, Papa, had landed on D-Day many years earlier. A World War II battle scene would never have been on my travel schedule in the past, but this was our trip and this spot was the one thing Derek wanted to see. It was only a few hours by train off our route, so how could I disagree?

"Here, take this with you." Months earlier, Papa had handed Derek a patch with an Indian head inside a star. Papa sat in his recliner in the living room of the assisted living facility in rural Colorado where he lived with his wife of sixty years, Eva. A retired physician, he'd served as a medic in the war. "It was from our infantry."

Derek looked down at the patch and wrote down a few numbers as Papa talked. The infantry division, platoon number, regiment—it all breezed through my brain, but Derek wanted to have his homework done when we got there. Papa was in his nineties, and though usually slow getting out of his recliner, he was mentally sharp, as able to make jokes about the current president as he was to recall the details of waiting in the boat to go up the beach.

"I was one of the oldest ones," he told us—already married, a trained physician when he'd enlisted. "Some of those boys lied about their age so they could go fight." His eyes watered. "We were all so seasick. We were delayed a day out there on the water because of the weather. Boys were throwing up over the sides." As he hunched over in his chair, I saw history alive in front of me.

A few years after that, my father-in-law would stand at the top of a ramp at Union Station in downtown Denver. He would point to it and tell me that was where he met Papa as a two-year-old boy. Where he met his daddy for the first time as he returned on the train from war. I imagined a young, handsome Papa walking up the ramp in his uniform, taking his boy in his arms. And a young Mama so relieved her doctor husband was home.

We carried our backpacks through the cobbled streets of Normandy to the youth hostel we'd emailed weeks earlier. Flags from around the world hung from the second stories of stone buildings. Later, as we walked to the center of town to book a tour for the next day, signs greeted us in windows. In English they read, "Veterans welcome here." Tours were based on language and country of interest. Those standing in line to purchase the German tours shifted their weight from side to side. We splurged and signed up for a small-group semiprivate tour for Americans.

"Do any of you have a personal connection?" the Frenchwoman driving the van called over her shoulder as she turned down the road that would take us toward the Normandy beaches. Her dark hair and obvious French accent reminded me of my father's girlfriend.

The three middle-aged couples who shared our van shook their heads. Based on their ages and collared dress shirts, I suspected they fit the profile of the typical tourists in this history-saturated town.

"My grandfather was here on D-Day," Derek spoke up. The attention in the van shifted toward us as the other couples stared at him, a little bit in awe.

"Oh! Did he come back for the anniversary?" Our tour guide talked to her rearview mirror as she drove. "I got to host a group of veterans for the week. It was *fantastíque*!"

"No. He came back. But not for the anniversary."

"Oh." She lowered her voice. "Well, tell your grandfather 'thank you' from us. We owe him our freedom. Do you know what regiment he was in?" The pep was back in her voice. "I could take you to where he landed."

My cynical side guessed her friendly nature was her attempt at a bigger tip at the end of the hour. But her enthusiasm didn't seem contrived. Maybe some French could tolerate Americans.

Pulling the piece of paper from months earlier out of his pocket, Derek started throwing out numbers. Our tour guide shook her head, saying, "*Non, non.*" I could tell Derek was frustrated, disappointed. He thought he'd written the numbers down just as Papa had said, but the tour guide insisted, "There was no regiment with that number."

Then Derek pulled the patch out of his pocket and handed it to her over the seat. "I have this."

She pulled the van to the side of the road and stopped, took the patch in her hand, and turned it over to reveal the Indian head symbol.

"Oohhh!" No need for translation, this universal exclamation said there was meaning behind what she held. The entire group was now looking at her with eyebrows raised, leaning in with expectation.

"This is for the 2nd Division. I know right where they landed."

I expected everyone in the van to start giving each other high fives. Papa was no longer just Derek's grandfather; within minutes he had moved into the position of van hero.

"Shall we go there?" she asked our group. There was no question as everyone nodded furiously. The tour had quickly changed to a personal interest story that we all wanted to claim as our own. Our tour guide did a U-turn, and we headed south along the rocky coastline.

In a way, Derek's story was becoming mine. And mine his. Our lives were not just crossing, they were melding, creating a new legacy built from both our histories. This trip was evidence of that. Unlike the other passengers in the van, I had a special claim on Papa's story. He was part of Derek, so in a two-lives-becoming-one kind of way, he was part of me.

Pulling halfway up a slope, our new French friend stopped the van and put the parking brake on. Turning around in her seat, she looked Derek directly in the eye.

"Here we are." She motioned to the van door with her hand. "They walked from the beach up this hill."

We looked out the window to see a small stone marker with the now familiar Indian head symbol on it. We climbed out of the van one at a time, and the wind wrapped around us and snapped of men who had died climbing on their bellies up the hill. Derek stretched his long legs out of the van and stopped. He looked down at the ocean below with its gray water and churning waves. He turned and looked up the hill with the grass blowing sideways. Tears began sliding down his cheeks, and he looked down at me. I smiled back between my tears.

The other members of our group stepped aside to clear a path between us and the stone mini-monument. Derek faced it with the ocean in the background, picturing his grandfather waiting an extra day past the breakers in the choppy water, scared for his life. He looked up the hill, imagining Papa crawling between downed soldiers to see if he could help.

It was a moment where history of country, family, and self came together and created a sacred place. I watched Derek's face and heard the rhythmic crashing of the waves in the distance.

There is a reason we say they stormed the beaches at Normandy. They didn't simply run or meander or stroll. They charged with a passion for country and freedom, knowing their lives would likely be sacrificed for a greater good. Standing on that hillside, I saw part of the legacy my future children would be born into.

Neither one of us wanted to get back in the van, but we were shivering from the wind. Our van mates were patiently waiting in the vehicle, watching us through the windows. A few of them wiped tears from their cheeks.

As we drove away, one of the other passengers, a rotund Midwestern kind of man, broke the silence. "Tell your grandfather 'thank you' from us too."

As I looked up at my husband, I thought I might explode from pride.

iii

FORGIVENESS

My father's girlfriend pulled her car into a driveway, and I heard the gravel crunch underneath. I'd been disappointed—and a little relieved—when we stepped onto the train station platform an hour earlier to find her standing there without my father.

"There wasn't enough room in the car for all of us" was her explanation as we tried stuffing our two backpacks into the shoebox-sized trunk of her tiny French car. "You have so many things," she commented as we pushed our bags down.

I tried not to be annoyed.

The gravel driveway circled a stone fountain, and beyond it was a three-story stone home that looked like it could be on the cover of a French travel brochure. The Loire River moved by slowly behind the house. If I wasn't feeling my heart race and my stomach turn a little, I'd have thought I'd arrived in a picturesque paradise.

Girls came running out. My baby sister was now six years old, with a two-year-old little sister of her own. Behind them walked my almost seventy-year-old father, looking more gray and frail than he did the last time I saw him.

We'd traveled a lot of miles to this French schoolhouse turned home and studio. To the moment when my husband would meet my father. Derek's height and broad shoulders were more noticeable as he unfolded himself from the French-sized minicar. As my father approached us, Derek stretched out his hand for a handshake.

"Hello. Nice. To. Meet. You." Derek directed his words with a loud staccato, as if the language barrier could be overcome with increased volume. I could tell Derek wanted to do right by me, defend me, stand up for me, look my father in the eye in an Old West kind of way to say that he knew. He knew that my father hadn't called for years at a time. That he pushed me aside like a disposable daughter. That he had other children he cared for more. I was proud of Derek's motives but wanted him to not be so big and loud. Not so American.

Despite my husband's chivalrous attempts, my father wasn't going to engage in a conversation about my childhood. Especially not right there on the gravel drive. Perhaps never. Besides, Derek's too much of a peacemaker, too charming to not warm up to anyone quickly. Within a few hours, he had two little French girls swinging from his American superhero arms.

The conversations in the days that followed were awkward as we discussed typical getting-acquainted topics: Derek's family, our jobs, where and how we met. These were conversations I could picture if we had been assigned to this family through a random foreign-study program, but not with my father and sisters. The disconnect between what was and what should have been made all of our words sound echoey, reverberating back to us, reminding us we were saying the right things, but to people who should have already known the answers.

We skipped around anything of substance, anything about my relationship with this foreign family, at least. Sitting at the lunch table after a savory meal of *coq au vin* and red wine, we talked about the French health care system and tax rate. About the amount of maternity leave a Frenchwoman qualified for and the child-care expenses that were covered while she worked.

As days went by, I displaced my unsettled feelings by becoming increasingly annoyed at a six-year-old who was throwing frequent fits. Now that I have my own children, I recognize my sister's multiple meltdowns as a combination of exhaustion from an interrupted schedule and the tension we brought with us into her home. At the time I found her to be simply spoiled.

"Why don't you go with her?" my father asked as my screaming sister pulled my sleeve to go up to our father's third-story bedroom.

It was four days into our stay, and she was feeling fully comfortable expressing herself with her foreign company. Our conflict had escalated over the last few minutes. I had no desire to see the bedroom he shared with a woman half his age and was a little annoyed that this six-year-old daughter of his thought she could boss me around. She got more agitated as she continued to plead, and I got more annoyed as I continued to say no.

Until our father stepped in and asked me to give in to her. My jaw dropped a little. Did anyone ever say no to this child?

"She is just a child," he reasoned.

"Just a child"? Did he really want to talk about "just a child"? To go there? I felt the blood rush to my head. How about a child who needed a father every day of her life? Who never threw a tantrum in front of him, not because she was perfect, but because he was never there to see it? A girl who needed affirmation that she was indeed beautiful, talented, and worth paying attention to? A girl who needed to hear that she deserved to be loved and to choose her relationships wisely? A girl who required wisdom, protection, and guidance from her father?

Really, "just a child"? I could tell him about "just a child." I wanted to scream it all at him. But I knew the six-year-old next to me didn't need to hear me say those things to her father. I wanted to protect her from the confusion of my own childhood, so I held it in.

The most maddening part was the disappointed look I felt he was giving me. A look that implied, *How could you treat this six-year-old girl so poorly? With such immaturity? Aren't you the adult here?*

I got up and stormed onto the balcony, where Derek sat watching the river.

"How did that go?" He'd overheard the power struggle the last few minutes. A struggle between sisters separated by twenty years in age, opposing cultures, different languages, and most blatant to me, different amounts of their father's attention. Derek's flippant tone told me he didn't understand the nuance involved. Flopping down in the chair next to him, I looked out at the river and seethed.

That night I slid under the covers of the antique queen bed in the guest room. My anger had tapered down to a low-grade fever of hurt. The grief that was underneath it bubbled up and took over. I slipped my arms around Derek and let his chest muffle my sobs.

"What's going on?" he started to ask, but stopped himself just as the words came out. There was no real answer because there was no definitive question. The grief was for what could have been, what should have been, and what would never be. We had passed the point of repair. I would never get the daddy from my childhood whom the girl in me still longed for. I had to know how to live in the shape I was in. To move forward with a husband who was willing to put his arms around me and hold me tight for as long as I needed. With a God who allowed the pain to be there and was always willing to love me through it. It didn't make sense, but it was time for me to be the grown-up and forgive.

A few days later, we pushed our backpacks into the trunk of the minicar to head back to the train station. As Derek said good-bye to the girls, my father pushed a roll of bills into my hand. "For your time in Barcelona," he said.

I wanted to squeeze out the words, "I forgive you," but I couldn't. I wasn't sure he thought he needed forgiveness, and I didn't want to stir up tension just as we were leaving. I wanted to be done. I would need to let the burdens fly off me in private. To let go of the anger for my sake, for my future family's sake, on my own. Forgiveness was about me letting go. It really had little to do with him.

A quick hug and a kiss on the cheek, and we were pulling out of the gravel driveway and then on the train to Barcelona, where Derek and I would sleep at my dad's apartment after staying out dancing until four in the morning. Where we'd have dinner with my former babysitter and her family and walk down La Rambla next to people who looked like they could be my cousins. Where we ate steaming calamari under the palm trees in the ancient Plaça Reial and drank espresso in cafés tucked between cobblestones in the Barri Gòtic, surrounded by the shadows of my ancestors and a cultural heritage I would never really know. Where I was ready to start living out of God's legacy. A legacy of forgiveness and love.

Section 5

Motherhood

i

Pregnancy

My hand began shaking, moving the pregnancy test it held, when the two blue lines appeared. At first faint, the lines grew stronger before my eyes. Like magic. Positive. Derek and I hugged and then jumped in the car to race to the drugstore for a backup test just to be sure. The second test confirmed we were expecting a baby.

It wasn't a practical time to start trying to expand our family. In fact, some might say it was irresponsible. Derek had quit his job a few months earlier to finish remodeling our fixer house, a Portland bungalow repossessed when the previous owner went to jail for dealing drugs from its back door. We took the bars off the windows and reclaimed it as a place of joy. Friends spent hours helping us rip up carpet, lay tile, and remove wallpaper. We got takeout for anyone who was on the crew, and it was months of laughter and gratitude.

Many of our Portland neighbors had nontraditional divisions of labor, and stay-at-home dads were not uncommon. But that's not what we'd planned, nor what I wanted. The thought of leaving our baby with anyone, including Derek, sounded like misery.

Since before we were married, I knew I wanted to be home full-time no matter the sacrifices. The decision to start "trying" when Derek had no income didn't make sense. But the maternal pull was strong, and we were surrounded by friends having babies, so I started paying close attention to my cycle, knowing it could take months to get pregnant. It only took two.

Five months after our positive test, I sat on the moving van bench, bouncing up and down as I read names to Derek from a baby name book, and willed my bladder to make it to the next stop.

The last few months had been filled with life-altering decisions. I thought my pregnancy would be consumed with lighthearted choices about nursery colors and stroller systems. But Oregon's job market was named the worst in the country, so we reversed the Oregon Trail as we made our way east toward the Rocky Mountains in a 2002 version of a covered wagon: a Penske moving van. We were headed to Denver and a job offer for Derek so I could start my new vocation as full-time mom. I was one big mess of opposing emotions: sad to leave what was behind and excited for what was ahead.

We pulled into my in-laws' driveway, the view of Boulder and the Continental Divide in the distance. For the two months that followed, their house was our temporary migrant camp, our possessions stacked in boxes in their garage, Derek's childhood bedroom our makeshift home with its high school basketball trophies on the shelves. Our two-month stint there made the baby in my belly the fourth generation to live on that property, my mother-in-law's parents having been real-life homesteaders there. Derek's parents, Lynn and Carol, made sure we knew we could stay in their basement as long as we needed.

The conflicting emotions continued: I felt welcomed but at the same time anxious to get my own spot. I was determined not to bring the baby home to Derek's basketball trophies.

"My grandchild!" Carol's enthusiasm for her first grandchild was evidenced by the greeting she often gave me—or, rather, she gave the baby in my belly—when I walked in the room. I cringed when she said it. I knew the words showed she was excited about her grandchild, but it felt like I'd morphed from a woman to a uterus with legs. I could have focused on the positive—her enthusiasm—but I didn't. I chose to let it sting. I wondered what it meant about my new status as mom. Is that how everyone would see me now? A baby machine? I didn't really think Carol did. But there was no question I had a new dimension that was part physical and very visible, and part so much more.

I was grateful Carol kept the fridge stocked with all my pregnancy-requested food, but unlike Derek, who was "home," I didn't feel like the fridge was mine to raid. Moving to Colorado was moving onto Derek's turf and further into my married family. A family with lots of cousins, aunts and uncles, and sisters. Real siblings with inside jokes about memories from years ago. Shared experiences and a bond I would never fully understand. And now I was the bearer of the first Kuykendall grandchild, and in some ways my identity shifted in this group from "Derek's wife" to include "mother of Derek's child." The shift was new for all of us, and we were trying to find our footing.

For two months while Derek and my in-laws went off to work, I went to Home Depot to buy supplies for our second round of a fixer house. The only home we could afford in the "up and coming" Denver neighborhood we hoped for had broken windows and grime and graffiti on the walls. Though the previous tenants had been a family of six, the house needed a complete overhaul to be considered habitable for our precious baby.

I heaved my pregnant body in and out of the car and through the heat to run errands so Derek could maximize his hours off his job doing projects at the house that I didn't have the energy or skill to do. Every evening we rendezvoused at our new house, and I watched him while he worked. Desperate for conversation, I followed him from room to room, avoiding deep breaths in case any harmful fumes might be lingering. Occasionally I panicked that the house would never be ready and went into cleaning mode, but the temperature, combined with my growing belly and the altitude adjustment, often left me breathless. So I sat and watched my husband, who in a frenzy of energy would put in a second shift as private contractor after his office day job. He was doing his best to provide for us with his own version of nesting.

"This isn't how I pictured it," I told Carol as I stood in her kitchen a few days later, trying to hold back the tears.

She smiled. "It never is. That's motherhood."

For some reason she found humor in what I said, and I found her response annoying. Maybe because it hinted that my life had plenty of other disappointments, unmet expectations, ahead. This was definitely not how I'd fantasized my months preparing for a baby. I wanted baby showers with tiny cupcakes and a nursery with gingham linens. I wanted foot massages from my husband and late-night ice cream binges. I was getting the late-night ice cream, thanks to a thoughtful mother-in-law, but everything else veered far off the romantic pregnancy bliss I'd imagined.

Our move-in date was moved up a month when I received a phone call from my doctor's office, telling me the blood test at my most recent appointment had come back positive for a condition that increased my chance of stillbirth. I needed to be induced a month early and closely monitored until then.

Holding the phone in my hand, I couldn't swallow, my heart racing. Another something not in my plan. Besides, our house would not be ready, the kitchen sink was on back order, and I was worried about the baby. I prayed that God would have mercy on all of us and deliver our baby safely into our arms.

ii

Delivery

I was induced at thirty-seven weeks because, as the doctor put it, my body was creating a "toxic environment." The baby needed to come out. But the same body that couldn't keep her was not ready to release her. Chemicals were used to start the labor process. It was many hours, long and exhausting. I knew ahead of time I wanted an epidural; I was too much of a wimp to do it any other way.

Yet when it came time to push, I was surprised at how much it hurt. If this was labor with pain medication, I couldn't imagine labor without it. The nurses kept asking me to make a distinction if what I was feeling was pain or just pressure. I wasn't sure. I'd never pushed a baby out before. Was "both" an acceptable answer?

"We need to remove your catheter to get ready for pushing," one nurse told me with an excitement in her voice that sounded forced, like she was trying to convince me that the pushing would be fun.

As she removed the catheter, I yelped in pain. I watched the nurse's eyes quickly lock with another's. "You felt that?" she asked with alarm in her voice.

Obviously, I thought. *Haven't you been listening to me?!* I could hear the screaming in my head, but I nodded silently.

"The epidural has worn off," the nurse announced to the room. It was the first of many nurse announcements I would hear that day. I was thankful for the affirmation that it did in fact hurt, but annoyed it took this long to get their confirmation.

"We can keep going or take a break to give you more relief."

"I want to stop," I whispered, though I wanted to scream, *Really? Is there any question? What crazy woman would keep going?*

"We'll need to get the anesthesiologist back in here."

The pushing was put on hold while the anesthesiologist was called out of surgery to put more chemicals in my body. Derek and my mom stood on either side of me, massaging my shoulders. I squeezed their hands until their fingertips looked like purple grapes.

Once the pushing started again, it was my turn to make an announcement. "I'm done! I can't go anymore." I was quitting. But even as I said it, I knew how dramatic it sounded and how impossible it was.

My mom got in my face to give me the pep talk, our noses just inches apart. "You can do this," she willed. If body-to-body transfer of energy was possible, she would have given me her every breath. I knew she was right. I had no other way out of this but to push. I kept going.

Fifteen hours after we started, the baby finally came out, and they announced we had a girl. My body was shaking from head to foot. Relieved the process was over, I was hardly curious about the baby. Wrapped in a pink and blue striped blanket, she was laid on my chest for just a second. I looked down to see the face of someone I didn't recognize. Her skin was red and her eyes were slits. As she blinked at the bright lights in the room, I could see dark coffee bean pupils. What could she possibly be thinking right then? That the world is too bright?

Because of my "toxic environment," my daughter was whisked away by the pediatric medical team for a full head-to-toe check.

Why was I shaking so much? I looked up at Derek, but his eyes were on the other side of the room with the baby. I shifted my eyes to my mom.

"You did it." She was crying and touched my forehead. I nodded. I had done it, and I was so glad it was over.

"Do you want to hold her?" A nurse returned with the swaddled baby burrito.

No, I didn't. I was afraid I would drop her with all the shaking, and there was a part of me that wanted nothing to do with the cause of all that had just happened the last several hours. Besides, I was wondering if she was really my baby. Why didn't I feel an instant recognition? That's what I'd pictured since the first time I thought of having a baby: that they would hand her to me and I would just know. I'd seen those baby reality shows, read the books—other people felt immediate connection. Shouldn't I be instantly drawn to her?

"You hold her," I mumbled to Derek. He held the wrapped bundle in his big man arms, walked over to the windowsill, and sat down on it facing me. I watched him bend over her and put his face next to hers. I was watching through water, with everything distant and unreachable. Even in that fog, the image of him gently holding her embedded itself in my brain.

The full-circle nature of that moment was not my first thought in my post-labor drugged daze. Watching Derek hold his new baby girl, our baby girl, was the promise of a new story. Of a new family structure. Of a father for my daughter. Despite my postpartum haze, my subconscious knew to capture that picture to remember forever.

Thinking back on my first meeting with my father, I can't help but think of my blue and white Dutch-style dress. And now my daughter's father was even a Dutchman. My last name, our last name, her heritage. No blue and white dress required. It was part of her blood. Her blonde hair and fair skin would later scream it. She had just come out of my body, but she was ours, both of ours, and we would do this together. I knew it in my soul.

Suddenly I knew I was going to be sick. My mom raised the baby-blue plastic hospital container to my chin, and I threw up for the third time that hour. The shaking wouldn't stop. And really, the delivery wasn't over. There was the placenta and the stitching, repairing the damage done to my privates in the process. I lay there wondering how much longer this could go on. I thought I was done when the baby came out. It was as though I had run a marathon and after crossing the finish line was told I needed to run just a few more miles to really be done.

For the next hour, the nurses kept offering me the baby to hold or try to nurse. I had no interest. I let my mom hold her, my mother-in-law, my sisters-in-law in the hall. I was not ready. And there was this growing feeling that something was not right. I should want to hold my baby.

Everyone else was happy and excited. I just wanted to sleep and be by myself. Finally a nurse said, "It's been an hour, and you *need* to hold your baby." She pushed the bundle toward me.

I had no choice but to put my arms out and take her. I was still operating underwater, and it all felt foreign. I looked down, hoping I would now recognize my daughter. "She doesn't look like either of us," I told Derek. "Who is she?"

To start with, she was a girl. That was a shock. Not because we'd had an ultrasound that indicated otherwise; we'd told our friends and family we wanted it to be a surprise on delivery day. But despite that public proclamation, in our minds we'd decided we were having a boy and we would call him Benjamin.

Derek, the only son of an only son, knew that his grandfather Papa, who'd stormed the beaches at Normandy, wanted us to have a boy. I knew because Papa told me outright when we got engaged years earlier that it was my responsibility to "get those boys out." A sweet man, already in his nineties when he gave me those instructions, he was able to be straightforward with what he wanted. His hopes and his death during my pregnancy probably impacted our expectations, as we imagined the doctor declaring, "It's a boy." Benjamin was now Gabriella. Gabriella, meaning "God is my strength." Gabi, our daughter.

I didn't hold Gabi for long. I passed her off, and the nurse announced it was time for me to move rooms. "You are too weak to walk. We'll take you in a wheelchair." She took one of my arms and instructed my mom to take the other, and they hoisted me into the chair. Taking the baby from whoever was holding her, the nurse announced, "This *mom* needs to hold her baby." She was calling me out, telling the world that it was obvious I didn't want to. But I was the mom, and I needed to step up and claim the title. I held on to the baby as Nurse Ratched pushed me through the maze of corridors to the room I would occupy for the next few days, barking her announcements along the way to strangers.

"Look at this mom. Didn't she do a good job?" I felt her pointing the spotlight on me as she pushed me through the halls, asking passersby to affirm me in my first identity crisis in motherhood.

We arrived in the room. Derek had gone ahead with armloads of pillows and bags filled with all of the things the pregnancy books told us we needed to take to the hospital but never touched. The ChapStick, the suckers, and the CD of calming music only served to make me feel prepared in the days prior. In this recovery room, the drugs would begin to wear off and the reality would begin to sink in: the baby had arrived safely, and I was now a mom.

The next few days in that hospital room, I felt increasingly better. The exhaustion and drugs started to wear off as I slept some. The hormones came to stay, though. The moods. The milk. Everything seemed to be wet and drippy. My tears. My breasts. My need for maxi pads.

The hospital is where the constancy of motherhood begins; there is no difference between night and day. The baby needs to be fed every two hours. The nurses flick on the lights in the middle of the night, making their nurse announcements about needing to check a vital sign or, worse, my stitches.

That first night the nurses took Gabi to the nursery. "You sleep now, while you can, and let her be with us for a few hours. We'll bring her in when she's hungry," they promised. The idea that Mom needs to take care of herself to take care of the baby had started during pregnancy. Eat the right things. Don't eat the forbiddens. Get sleep. Avoid stress. Drink water. Continue to exercise. Take care of yourself so you can take care of the baby. Now the baby was out, no longer part of my body, and the nurse was telling me the same thing. Take care of yourself so you can take care of the baby.

And so I slept. After what seemed like only five minutes, the light came on. *Really? It can't be time.* But I heard the cry. The newborn cry that sounded so frantic, so awful to my ears, and made me sit straight up. I now *knew* she was my baby. My eyes started to tear, and I wanted to protect her, to stop that awful, painful scream. There was relief in my response too. I *felt* like the mom. That bond must have been in there somewhere, because I couldn't wait to hold her. I thanked God that something in my heart had clicked, had been opened, to know I'd been created for this.

I looked over at Derek, who was still adjusting to the blinding light in the room. Didn't he hear his baby's cry? How scared she sounded? He didn't seem to get it. He wasn't jolted up like I was.

"She's hungry," the nurse announced, and we started the new foreign process of trying to nurse. This thing that was supposed to be so natural but in reality was so awkward. By that point I'd lost all sense of modesty. The gown came off, the pillows were arranged, and I tried to get that sweet but squawking baby to latch on. I was sweating. I needed her to stop crying. I wanted to do this right. I wanted to give her what she needed.

I'd uncovered a new kind of love. A love that surpassed anything I'd ever felt before. It consumed me from my bed head to my delivery-pedicured toes. I was the mom. I didn't come to that realization in the way I'd expected, but the result was the same: a mother was born.

iii

HORMONES

A week later, standing in the park-and-ride lot where suburban commuters parked and caught buses to the city's center, I held on to my mom and didn't want to let go. I'd spent the last ten years trying to separate from her, to be independent, different, and now all I wanted was for her to stay and take care of me. It was time to say good-bye, for her to take a shuttle to the airport to go home to Larry in Seattle, and for me to start life as a mom. Knowing how sad she was to leave, I tried not to cry. I blinked back the tears. The good-bye was inevitable, so I pulled my body from hers, stepped back, and opened the door of the car where Gabi and Derek waited.

As we drove away, Derek said, "I can't believe your mom. She's willing to take a bus to the airport."

"She's taken buses all over the world," I reminded him. I now let the tears flow freely and didn't bother wiping them since everything was already drippy and wet. They added to my generally moist state.

"I know, but still, she's so adventurous."

I wondered if I would always miss her this much.

For some reason, getting out of the house with the baby had turned a five-minute process into a forty-minute tactical exercise. So we were late, rushing from dropping off my mom at the shuttle stop to Lindsay's Colorado wedding reception at my in-laws' home. Derek's sister lived and got married in California, and we all assumed I would still be pregnant at this second reception. My early induction put me one week postpartum and a big weepy mess for the day. I spent the entire party hiding in my in-laws' bedroom, trying to nurse the baby while well-wishers came in to catch a peek. I eventually moved my hiding place to their bathroom until we left the party early.

Four days of sleepless nights and nap-filled days passed, and Derek went back to work. I spent nine hours holding the baby, putting her down only to toast a bagel and go to the bathroom. The reality of our move from Portland, and the loneliness it brought, was settling in. I had no one to call. One of my sorority sisters lived in Denver, but her days were consumed with graduate school. I didn't want to call my mom; it would just make both of us sadder. So I sat and wondered if this was what the rest of my life held.

It took about a week of that moping misery before I broke down at dinner.

"This isn't what I thought it would be," I told Derek, my legs stretched out from my chair to his.

"What's wrong?"

Staring at him, I didn't have an answer, and at the same time it seemed so obvious. That everything was wrong. It was nothing and everything at the same time. I started crying and couldn't stop. He wanted me to love being home with the baby. I wanted to love being home with the baby. My brain knew this was what I'd wanted since I first started thinking about creating my own family, to be fully consumed by motherhood. And yet I was sad and disappointed. I didn't know why I wasn't loving every second. I didn't know what was wrong with me.

A month later, Lindsay called from California. "I can't believe how much I miss that baby," she told Derek. So she bought a ticket and came to visit. The baby and I drove half an hour to Boulder to have lunch with Lindsay and Carol at a deli.

"You guys stay here," Carol said, motioning to the booth we'd chosen. "I'll go up and order. What would you like?"

I stared at the menu scribbled out on the chalkboard above the counter. It seemed like an impossible decision.

"A Cobb salad. No onion," Lindsay answered.

I looked at her in disbelief. How did she make that decision so quickly? With such confidence? And it sounded so healthy, so unsatisfying. Carol turned to me. I looked up at the board again and tried to block out the restaurant's background noise so I could focus.

"Can I hold her?" Lindsay asked as her mom walked to the counter to order. I watched Lindsay unbuckle the car seat, pull the baby up close to her face, and talk to her in a hushed voice. The cloud from labor and delivery had returned, putting everything I saw in a misty fog. Lindsay pulled her face back a few inches so she and the baby had full view of each other. I noticed Gabi follow her auntie with her eyes. Lindsay gave her a big smile, and then with a stab to my heart, Gabi smiled back. A huge cheek-to-cheek smile that flashed only for a second, but was without question a real smile, not just a facial spasm.

"Did you see that?!" Lindsay's voice indicated she was excited. And who wouldn't be? It was about the cutest thing the world had ever seen. "Has she ever done that before?"

"A few times," I answered, followed by, "I think." I couldn't really remember if or how many times Gabi had thrown out such an obvious smile. I wondered why my sister-in-law was better at getting my baby to smile than I was.

At home that afternoon, I lay Gabi on my bed and sat down next to her. She looked up from the flowered bedspread and kicked her jammied feet. I wondered if I should try to bend down and put my face close to hers, like Lindsay did earlier, and try to make her smile. I was terrified it wouldn't work, so I didn't try. If I tried and failed, it would confirm my biggest, most shameful fear: that I shouldn't be Gabi's mother. That my sister-in-law, who'd only been with the baby an hour, was better at caring for Gabi and making her feel loved than I was. *Maybe she should be Gabi's mom*, I thought.

I cried and wondered why motherhood was so completely different from what I had pictured. Why I was so sad when it was what I had wanted for so long. I now had the tight, clean, nuclear family I'd dreamed of, and all I wanted to do was sleep.

By the time Gabi was three months old, I was feeling more capable, more the person I remembered before delivery—well, really since before pregnancy. It was as though I'd had terrible PMS for three months. Once out of it, I could look back and see with some clarity that my hormones were dictating my feelings and behavior. A heavy case of the baby blues, I figured.

Years and another baby later, I heard a psychiatrist speak to a room of MOPS women on the topic of postpartum depression. As he listed off the symptoms, those first few months of mothering rushed back. Knowing depression is not neat and tidy but tends to fall on a continuum of symptoms, I realized I may have been further down the depression scale than I'd realized after Gabi was born. My bad case of the baby blues was more likely a mild case of postpartum depression. He then said something that made total sense: the development of postpartum depression is usually linked to a woman's perception of her support system.

"Remember, this is perception we're talking about," he said. "She may have a great support system to tap into, but if she doesn't believe she does, she'll feel isolated, and that will put her at risk."

I thought of the endless days sitting alone on the couch, nursing the baby, wondering if or how the next day would be any better. Of my prayers echoing off the walls of our tiny living room, bouncing back unanswered. Of daydreaming about the idyllic mothering life if only we still lived in Portland surrounded by sweet friends with babies. Of my mother-in-law and the women from her Bible study who brought me dinner and would have been thrilled to help more if only they, and I, knew I needed it. I likely had a support system available to me, but often perception becomes reality. I felt lonely and isolated, so I was lonely and isolated.

iv

Rocking

For all that lonely, silent time, I had lots of time to think. About what I wanted. What I had. What I didn't. Lots of time to feel what it was to be a mother and let it sink in to shape and change me. How many hundreds of times did I sit on our green oversized sofa and nurse Gabi to sleep? I would draw her to my breast, sit back in the velour pillows, and think and pray.

One afternoon, just as I was starting to come out of the three-month fog, I sat on the sofa for the fourth time that day, nursing the baby. I looked down at my sweatpants and wrinkled T-shirt and wondered if the unidentified odor I smelled was coming from me. The pile of dirty dishes in the sink were a room away, but they were at the forefront of my mind. Because the brain haze was clearing, I was getting anxious about getting some things done. Or at least I was more motivated to get dressed before noon. I'd already failed in that goal for the day. In fact, I hadn't done anything "productive" in the last week. How was it that one day was melting into the next, I was wearing the same clothes, and not one chore was getting checked off my to-do list?

I'm not doing anything! I thought. And with a gentle flash, I felt God's voice press down on me. *You don't need to do anything.* The feeling came on so quickly and was so against my performance nature that I felt it was certainly a Holy Spirit whisper to my soul. A rush of understanding that God created babies to need to eat every few hours and created mothers a distinct way in order to feed them. That nursing is God's gift to mothers because it forces us to slow down and savor the early weeks and months with our babies. That feeding Gabi was an incredibly productive job. And that my value didn't rest in my to-do list anyway. My job was to love God and Gabi while sitting on the sofa. That was it.

I felt God's love for my uncombed, smelly, sedentary self and agreed he probably didn't care if the dishes got done that afternoon. I understood all of this in an instant, and that this was only one of many object lessons motherhood would hold. Tiny, mundane things would represent God's great love for me in unexpected moments.

I'd already experienced one of those unforgettable moments. Despite the fog of the first few months, I distinctly remember sitting in the rocking chair in Gabi's room a week after bringing her home. It was Papa's rocking chair. He'd died only months earlier, and with our recent move to Colorado, we'd inherited some of his furniture.

I sat rocking back and forth, the repetitive motion comforting both of us. The light in the room was starting to dim as the sun went down outside, and my toes in their flip-flops pushed down on the floor, rocking the chair back and forth. Gabi was wrapped in a blanket, her tummy full from just eating. I had nowhere else to be but in that chair, rocking.

I thought about how much I loved her after only days of knowing her. For years I'd imagined what it would feel like to love my baby, and I was still unprepared for how pure and selfless it was. Looking down at the dark newborn hair on the top of her head nestled on my chest, I thanked God again for such a perfect gift.

The phrase "I would stand in front of a bus for her" flew through my mind. I laid a gentle kiss on her head and thought, *Yes, I really would step in front of a bus for this person. I would rather die than have her suffer. I would rather take her place.* Just as God took my place on the cross. How many times had I heard, "Once you have a child of your own, you better understand God's love for you"? It was true. This idea of unconditional love, no conditions, nothing that would change how pure and consistent it was—I had never experienced anything like it before.

Even my love for Derek was tied up in expectations of what a spouse should do. Marriage is two imperfect people bending toward each other, and I let my selfish needs get in the way too often of loving him selflessly. But this tiny baby, the love I felt after knowing her for only a matter of days, had changed me in a new way. I couldn't expect anything in return because she couldn't give it. She was absolutely dependent on me loving her without condition.

Back and forth I rocked, praying in silence. No words coming out of my mouth, but my soul singing praise. Thanking God for an inkling of the depth of his love. For letting me experience what it was to love another person without conditions. For letting me understand his love for me with new clarity. I couldn't give God much. What did I have that he needed? Nothing, really. He loved me—loves me—because he chooses to.

Back and forth I rocked, and I thought of my own mother. How this was a glimpse of her love for me. The tensions of growing up and making different decisions than she would have made slid into the background, because in the foreground was a better understanding of the depth of her love. I thought of her in her apartment in Barcelona, alone, rocking me as a baby, and wondered how that felt. Just the two of us, preparing to take on the world. I thought of her packing her bags with a toddler and again with an eight-year-old for an overseas move. Rocking Gabi, I better understood my mother's motives. I felt a new sympathy for her decisions and a new appreciation of how much she'd shaped me. For how much she loved me.

Back and forth I rocked, and I thought about my father. We hadn't spoken since he'd called a year earlier, September 12, 2001. The day after our nation's collective heart was broken. I'd stood in our Portland house holding the kitchen phone and heard the familiar delay of the overseas call. "The world is behind America. We are with you," he told me, neither of us knowing what the world had in store in the years, or even days, to come. Though brief, it was one of the more tender conversations we'd ever share. He recognized my American side without hinting of distaste. And for a moment he acknowledged my insecurity.

Back and forth I rocked. He didn't know we'd moved to Denver or that I had been expecting a baby. I wondered how he would feel, knowing I had a daughter. I felt a sadness that surprised me, because it wasn't a sadness for me, it was for him. Did he feel this kind of love for me when I was a baby? If so, what had kept him away? How could he possibly have stayed away? It seemed like a God-given wiring that I loved Gabi this much. I pictured her on the other side of the world, and my heart ached at the thought of that distance. Another phrase came to mind: "Going to the ends of the earth." Again, yes, I would go to the ends of the earth for this baby. I imagined myself in a fur-trimmed hooded parka, trekking through the blowing snow to get to an igloo to reunite with my lost child. Maybe I would never understand what kept him away.

Back and forth I rocked Gabi, and I promised her I would love her always.

Section 6

Friendship

i

Longing

"I brought copies of the recipe for these cookies," our class facilitator shouted above the room's chatter. Sitting on the plastic exercise mat with Gabi lying in front of me, I looked around at the other women. Each one had her baby in front of her, a matching set of mother and child. My eyes skimmed their faces, and I wondered if any could be a treasured friend, a "bosom friend," as Anne of Green Gables referred to her Diana.

I wanted a bosom friend. I missed having friends who knew me, women who knew I liked cream in my coffee, that I wore sweaters because I was always cold, that I was allergic to cats. Women with shared histories, experiences, who knew me before I was a mom, knew that I could be witty, that despite my recent wrinkled appearance, I did in actuality know how to iron, and that my Spanish was better than my Italian. That I didn't have to explain where or how I met my husband because they knew him and loved him too.

Looking around the room, I couldn't tell if anyone had bosom-friend potential or was even looking for it in the same way I was. We were in a classroom on the maternity floor of Saint Joseph Hospital in Denver. A few months had passed since my postpartum haze, and I was starting to move from a low-level state of desperation to a low-level handle on baby care. The facilitator for this new mom class had two kids, ages two and four, so as far as we were all concerned, she was a certified expert in all things mothering.

"It calls for whole wheat flour and natural sweetener," she half-yelled above the room's chatter.

I took a bite of my cookie and thought it was tasty, but an Oreo would be better. I wondered what she'd think if she knew I had a Snickers bar in my purse. A king-sized one.

The moms grabbed copies of the cookie recipe as it was passed around and studied it intensely while nodding their heads in approval. They wanted everyone to know they agreed it looked like the makings of an excellent, nutritious snack that only a mother could whip up. We were all there to get a recipe for successful mothering, and the cookie recipe was the closest we'd received yet, so we took it very seriously.

Every Wednesday morning, this group met for an hour and a half. Because the group was for new mothers with babies up to six months of age, it was fluid with the veterans aging out and newly terrified moms arriving weekly. I don't suppose it was an accident that the woman who led the group was not only a mom but also a hospital social worker. We were a desperate group of women and only half-jokingly said we needed professional help. Each meeting we'd discuss a topic, like healthy snacks, for half an hour and then move into the part we'd all been waiting for: time to talk to the women on either side of us.

It was like the beginning of recess on a playground; once granted permission for free time, we scrambled to get going and not waste a single second of potential conversation. The questions came out with such speed we forgot to breathe in between.

"Did your baby get her three-month shots yet? Are you going back to work? Are you happy about that? Have you been pumping?

What brand of diapers absorbs the best? What brands are on sale at King Soopers this week?" Anything, really, that would be a connection point. That would give us insight into navigating days with a newborn and help us assess if there was a potential friend in the women sitting around us. Anything that would say we were alike, that we weren't crazy. Anything that would affirm we were doing it right.

I came to the group via the one mommy friend, Jennifer, who'd plopped into my life. The weekend we pulled the moving van into my in-laws' driveway, Derek and I went to a party in Denver at his friend Brian's house. Brian had gone to graduate school with Derek in Portland and moved to Denver with his bride, Crystal, a year earlier. I didn't know them, but I already missed friends back home and figured a party was better than unloading the moving van.

Jennifer and I were both pregnant, sitting on Brian and Crystal's front porch, appreciating the cool the evening offered. My swollen feet were wedged into my flip-flops, glad to be getting a break from holding up the extra weight my petite frame was carrying. Neither of us knew anyone other than our husbands and the party's hosts, so we found refuge in each other's pregnancy war stories. Jen was outgoing—what I needed to make that conversation happen—and funny. It was good to laugh with someone, and at the end of the night when we exchanged phone numbers, I assumed she had a whole slew of girlfriends who took up her allotted friend hours.

But then a few weeks later she called. And I called her back. Just a few conversations as our due dates approached, but they were an unexpected gift. A dating relationship of sorts. It felt nice to be pursued. A few weeks after our babies were born, the frequency of the phone calls increased. It didn't take long to stop feeling like I didn't have anyone to call. A social worker as well, Jen began to find resources for us like we were her two neediest clients. She found every puppet show and mommy-and-me swim class in the greater metro area. I hated going to the freezing pool, but I lived for getting out of the house, so I followed along. Where Jen went, I went. Our baby girls, just ten days apart, shared their developmental milestones. Their mommies did too.

Jen found out about the class at Saint Joseph Hospital. Desperately lonely with a completely open schedule, I signed up. Each week I pushed the stroller through the maze of hospital hallways back to the car with an air of disappointment. Jen seemed to be making other friends. I wasn't jealous of her new friendships, just of the ease with which she made them. She was becoming my dearest companion, but she had a life; she couldn't be my everything. I knew it was good for everyone if I had more friends, it was just that the effort required seemed forced. I'd always connected with others naturally through things I was already part of—work, church, other friendships. Being new to Denver, I didn't bring those pre-baby connections with me. The only thing I had in common with these women were babies the same age, and that wasn't enough. I needed more because I was more.

Each week as I walked back to the parking garage, I thought about my crew back in Portland, imagining what they were doing. As I strapped Gabi into her car seat, I wondered if my introverted nature was getting in the way of making friends. Maybe if I asked more questions, I'd get past the diaper discussions. Despite my disappointment, as soon as I pulled my seat belt strap across my chest, I started counting the days until the next Wednesday, hopeful next week might be the week I made a connection.

ii

Comparisons

I looked at Gabi chewing on the plush toy that belonged to Carrie's baby, Logan. Not sure how Logan's mom would react to the germ sharing, I glanced over at her. She was deep in explanation about their recent house remodel. Ten of us from the hospital group decided to keep our weekly meeting times. All first-time moms, we needed a place to ask questions and normalize the sleep-deprived, hormone-driven life we were leading. It was Carrie's turn to host the group, so all of the babies were exploring her toy selection.

Gabi had recently learned to sit up, but Logan, only a month older, was toddling around her. Logan's hair looked so put together—the bows holding up her chocolate-colored curls matched her coordinated outfit. I looked at Gabi. Her almost white blonde hair was growing out like Bozo the Clown's, almost nothing on top and long around the base of her head. Her pink flowered pants and green striped shirt would never be considered an "outfit." Looking at Carrie again, the mother in the well-coifed pair, I wondered how long it took her to do her hair in the morning. I examined her part, impressed that she could make a ponytail look like a hairstyle. I was sure I could never get a ponytail to look that good.

"You know my husband's in construction, so he just laid the foundation for the add-on." She was pointing to the large bedroom added onto the back of the kitchen. I wondered how it felt to be married to someone in construction. To have a new master bedroom. To have hair that looked like it was straight from the salon. Though I was starting to get to know the women in the group, I was often using our time together as a way to escape into their lives and, as a result, find dissatisfaction in mine. Everyone seemed to have something different, better, than I did. A nicer house, better vacations, a husband who made more money. Despite my generally confident nature, my insecurities were the only thing I seemed to have more of.

I left every week wondering why we talked so long about diaper rash cream and so little about things that mattered. Well, things that mattered to me: why I loved my baby so fiercely, how I apologized to Derek for being too quick to flash anger, what I cried about in the middle of the night. It wasn't a safe place to be vulnerable, so I let my insecurities take over, and inside my head it got ugly. Feeling like I had loftier topics to cover made me feel deep, but really I was just self-righteous.

A month rolled around, and it was my turn to host the group again. I started preparing days ahead. Shopping for the snacks. Wiping down the baseboards. Cleaning the toilet. Tasks I was able to overlook for months at a time had a sudden urgency. Why didn't I have ten matching glasses? Why hadn't Derek painted the trim in the basement yet? Why was my house so small? I felt nauseous at the thought of Amy seeing my college futon as our basement sofa. I thought of her remodeled playroom and wanted to stomp my feet.

Don't do that, I told myself. *You have a husband who loves you and a healthy baby. You shouldn't care about what your house looks like. You are lucky to have a house.* The self-talk worked for a few minutes. I remembered Erica, whose townhome was smaller than mine, and Courtney, whose husband traveled all week for work, and my comparisons would stop. But it was a short-term fix; the long-term issues didn't go away. I wasn't satisfied with what I had. I was comparing, and it left me wanting more.

A few weeks later, I drove out of the city to the suburbs south of Denver. Courtney had moved out of her cottage in Wash Park to a new house, one with more space, and we were all meeting there for the first time. As I drove through the suburban neighborhood, I wondered how anyone my age could afford such luxury. It felt so adult, like places where people older, more grown-up, lived. I was getting farther down my list of directions, which meant I was getting closer to my final destination, and the houses were getting bigger and nicer with each turn. I opened the back car door to get Gabi out of her car seat, and the scratch on the door caught my attention.

As I walked up to the house, I considered turning around to go home. This wasn't good for me, this always wanting what I didn't have. But I'd been counting the days for the social time, and I wasn't about to miss it. The front door was open, and the chatter from the women who'd already arrived was floating out onto the front porch. Stepping inside, I found an empty, carpeted living room to my right and a formal dining room to my left. I followed the voices and stepped into a showroom-like kitchen. Courtney was standing behind the island talking in her usual animated way, arms flailing as she told a story of her latest girls' weekend away. My eyes went around the kitchen to the cherry cabinets, the stainless steel appliances, the granite countertops, and I thought, *She doesn't even like to cook.*

Courtney saw me out of the corner of her eye. "Oh, hey, Alex. Come on in." She was genuinely gracious. "Put your bag anywhere, we're just going to hang out on the floor. I've ordered the new furniture, but it's not here yet." She waved her hand in the direction of the playroom off the kitchen. I looked over to see familiar mom and baby faces already sprawled on the floor and catching up from the week apart. I saw Carrie and her great hair. I lifted my hand to my head and tried to smooth my hair. Why was it so frizzy? Neither straight nor curly, it didn't offer me much. I looked down at my jeans. The term "mom jeans" was probably created after someone saw me. I wanted to disappear. Nothing seemed enough. My house. My car. My hair. My clothes.

I propped Gabi in a sitting position on the cream carpet and let the diaper bag slide down my arm onto the floor next to her. Logically I knew these thoughts weren't true. I was more than the sum of my stuff. I was created in God's image. To be made to reflect the Creator was not something I blew off. But it was hard to absorb, to internalize and live from. Especially when there were cabinets and jeans and SUVs taunting me at every turn, saying, "She has more, she's worth more."

I turned back toward the kitchen and listened to Courtney talk about the all-inclusive resort in Mexico she'd visited two weeks earlier. I indulged in the thought of a vacation by the pool. No baby needing to be changed or held. I knew I didn't really want to go on vacation without Gabi, but for just a minute, the idea of a magazine and a froufrou drink with an umbrella and friends from college sounded wonderful. I smiled as I realized my mini daydream was the closest to a vacation like that I'd have in a long time, if ever.

Courtney must have seen me out of the corner of her eye again because she stopped midsentence and turned to me. "Alex, you look so great!"

The other women standing around the island turned in unison and looked me up and down to see if they agreed.

"Uh, thanks?" If only she knew the internal dialogue, the insecurities, the obsession with the outward appearance I'd been having. The lack of confidence about the package I presented.

"You're always so put together," she said as she turned back to her audience to finish her story.

My smile widened. Really, if only she knew.

iii

Judging

A few weeks later, we sat in the basement of Amy's Wash Park house. Wash Park is the locals' term for Washington Park, a neighborhood Derek and I had driven through for fun when we moved, knowing nothing in that zip code would fit in our budget. The group had already met a handful of times at Amy's house, so I wasn't shocked that day by the craftsman furniture that matched her 1920s bungalow, but I couldn't help but calculate in my head how much each piece must have cost.

"I found a day care for Justin," she announced to the group.

I could tell by the excitement in her voice she was happy about that. I looked at Gabi drooling in the middle of the mommy circle, other babies climbing over her, and was grateful I didn't have to hand her over to anyone else for the day. I pictured a sterile room with dirty toys, seven kids screaming, and two women trying to manage it all, and I had an internal shudder. I couldn't understand why Amy would be so anxious to get back to work.

"I'll just be going back three days a week." Three days a week sounded like a lot. "And we need the money." It rang of justification. A reason no one could deny: the need for money.

The new can lights in her recently remodeled basement shone down on us. *Need?* I thought. *How about going without? What is "need" anyway?* I knew I was judging her, but I didn't care. I thought of all the penny pinching that went into my every decision, big or small: what was for dinner, whether I could visit my mom, if I could go out for coffee, the brand of diapers I bought. We didn't have cable or cell phones or new clothes. We were sacrificing so I could raise our daughter. How dare she say she needed the money!

Jen and I made eye contact over the pile of babies. Her face didn't move, but our eyes reassured each other. *Stay strong, sister. You're doing the right thing,* and a little bit of, *And she is not. For shame.*

Now, ten years of mothering behind me, I am embarrassed at how quick I was to judge another mom's decision. But I did. And on certain topics I judged frequently. It was because my choices were based on my values. Values I desperately clung to. Starting a family of my own, I was in control of how it would look. I was determined to do it the right way. I would give all of myself to my child. All of my attention. All of my time. All of my resources. She would never question whether I was there for her. Even if that meant smothering her.

So if another mom made a different choice, it was because she was operating under a different value system. Or at least that's what it felt like. And that felt threatening because I had a lot at stake. I couldn't offer room for ambiguity because that meant there wasn't a right way, and I needed there to be a right way. One right way.

Just like when I was a high school student who wanted a formula for success, a perfect combination of required and extracurricular courses, I wanted a mothering formula. And one I could be graded on that would give me a chance for that 4.0. To affirm my value as a mother. Those perfectionist tendencies were creating a need to compare myself to others, making me competitive and self-righteous.

My pastor, Steve, says if you are good at following the rules, at performance, you run the risk of becoming proud. And that's where

I was. Following rules that I thought pointed to the right way to mother, the best way, the most sacrificial way. And I was priding myself on it. I was judging others, walking around with an invisible measuring stick and comparing all of my measurements. My motives weren't malicious; in fact, I usually didn't realize I was doing it. I can see now I was merely trying to figure out where I stood in the world. Saying there was a right way to mother and following the rules gave me something to cling to, a misplaced security.

Six months later, I walked into a MOPS group meeting at Corona Presbyterian Church in Denver and met the group's coordinator, Julie. We'd talked on the phone the week before and discovered a Pacific Northwest connection. Her parents and sister lived on Whidbey Island. She understood my coffee-drinking, ferryboat-riding side, and it felt like a taste of the friendships I'd left in Portland. I didn't need to introduce those parts of me; she already understood them.

"We're about to break for the summer, but come anyway. We're really laid-back," she'd said on the phone.

Still desperate for some friends, I thought this group could introduce me to moms beyond my weekly Wednesday playgroup. My phone call with Julie confirmed I might have a connection.

Though she was ten years older, Julie looked like she could be my sister with her dark hair and short stature. She had grown up a pastor's daughter, but she didn't fit my stereotype of a prim, quiet church lady. She was boisterous and direct in her communication. A mother of three—her youngest child being the same age as Gabi—she was tying up her baby years as I was diving in. I watched as she went out of her way to make other moms feel comfortable, me included.

My assumption about being a mom, a grown-up, in the church was doing things a certain way, based on the right answers. Julie openly questioned everything. About mothering. About church. About why God said certain things in the Bible. I didn't quite know how to respond. She'd grown up in church. I hadn't. She must have known if she was out of line.

Once when our MOPS group had a counselor come and speak about self-care, the conversation turned to our children's fathers. An equally outspoken and candid woman sitting next to Julie raised her hand to share.

"I feel like my husband only wants sex from me. And he feels like the only reason I stay with him is for his money."

Julie, sensing an opportunity for a joke, turned to her neighbor and responded so the room could hear, "So what you're saying is, you get paid to have sex?"

Laughter exploded from the other fifty women in the room. I skimmed the crowd to see if anyone was offended by her comment. No one seemed to be. Although I was a little stunned at these two women and their openness—they knew we were in a church basement—I was also relieved. A release from the formula of what I needed to be and say. I was still stuck in those Christian rules for living from so many years earlier, which fit right into my drive for perfection. I walked into this church group thinking I would have to censor my conversation, when in reality there was more freedom. Less comparison. Less judgment.

In Philippians, Paul writes,

> Steer clear of the barking dogs, those religious busybodies, all bark and no bite. All they're interested in is appearances—knife-happy circumcisers, I call them. . . . The very credentials these people are waving around as something special, I'm tearing up and throwing out with the trash—along with everything else I used to take credit for.[2]

Circumcision—not something I've dealt with as a mom of girls. But in the Bible, it represented a rule, an outward appearance, that showed religious compliance, doing things the right way. I had unknowingly become a knife-happy circumciser. Someone running around with scissors, wanting to cut all of the wrong things out of my life. My credentials of performance—of being a stay-at-home mom who cooked a real dinner every night, who was financially responsible, and who went to church on Sundays—were what I pushed forward first for everyone to see. I was allowing what I was doing, and doing the right way, to define me. But it didn't leave much room for authenticity. I could be honest about the parts of my life that were going well, but I'd catch myself censoring conversations when they were in areas of insecurity.

Julie had already torn up her credentials and thrown them in the trash like Paul. She'd been divorced and pregnant when she got married the second time. When her husband met her parents—a retired pastor and his wife—for the first time, he and Julie also announced the news of her pregnancy. Julie said her mom jumped up, hugged her, and said, "You're going to be a mom!"

"That could have been embarrassing for her, me being the pastor's daughter and all," Julie told me. "But that's who she was. She was excited for me and didn't focus on what I did. She focused on what God was doing."

I was searching for the grown-up rules. I found Julie and her confidence to be invigorating. Rather than needing to prove she was good enough in mothering, she trusted in God's amazing grace. I wanted to live with the same freedom she did. Less concerned with how things appeared and more concerned with how they actually were. I just couldn't shake the need for a playbook. That rule-following part of me that had always been there followed me straight into motherhood.

But right there in the playbook of life, the one I thought had all the rules I was supposed to follow, Paul says:

> I didn't want some petty, inferior brand of righteousness that comes from keeping a list of rules when I could get the robust kind that comes from trusting Christ—*God's* righteousness.[3]

Righteousness—a word that means always behaving by the moral code. On its own it sounds religious, judgmental. What I didn't realize is the Bible, the playbook, was saying let go. Let go of the rules. Of the expectations, of the list of "shoulds," of the outward appearance, and know Jesus. Plain and simple, know him and trust him.

Section 7

Coming into My Own

i

My Baby—Myself

"We've decided she likes it best when I am holding her and she is looking at Daddy," I told Carol. We were at my mother-in-law's house, and I was sitting on a stool at the bar in her kitchen, watching her prep dinner for us. Gabi sat on my lap facing her Oma and kicking and flailing her arms up and down with joy.

"She thinks you're just an extension of her, like an arm. Daddy is clearly someone else." Carol held the knife midair for a moment as she thought about what she'd just said. It gave me pause too. Gabi did think I was an extension of her. A set of breasts to feed her, arms to pick her up when she cried, her need-meeter at every turn. She was happiest when I held her. When Derek tried to take her from me, she'd lean her body, her arms outstretched in my direction, so it was just easiest if I held her all the time.

And I was starting to wonder if she was an extension of me. I'd never spent so much one-on-one time with another person. Well, maybe my own mother when we moved to Italy, but that was only for a few months while we traveled before I went off to school and she went to work. Gabi was now ten months old, and

I didn't go anywhere that she didn't go except for the single dentist appointment I'd had since her arrival. Even at my postpartum visit to my obstetrician, Gabi screamed in her car seat on the floor next to the exam table while my feet were in the stirrups.

She went with me to the bathroom, to the bank, to bed, to the grocery store. I was wondering where I ended and where she started. But that's what I'd wanted. I didn't want to leave her with anyone. At the same time, I was exhausted and dreamed of time by myself.

A week earlier, I'd looked up from the kitchen sink and found Derek unraveling his earphones while walking toward the back door.

"I'm going for a run," he said, his eyes focused on his earphone wires, his running shorts and shoes on. I felt my anger instantly flare at his announcement that he was off to do his own thing for the next hour while I stayed at home. Again. With no one but a baby to talk to. All week I'd waited for him to come home, and he was leaving, making my weekend look like an extension of my week.

"Fine," I replied.

He stopped midstep and turned to face me. "Is there a problem with that?"

"No," I lied.

"Okay. Fine. I'll be back in an hour."

"Fine," I said as he turned toward the door.

He stopped midstride again and turned back around. Tired that the tone of my voice was not matching the words coming out. "What's the problem?" he asked.

"Well, why did you think you could just leave?"

"Do you have something you need to do? Besides, the baby's asleep."

"Just this"—I flicked my hand toward the dishes in the sink—"but you leaving without asking implies I'm always on baby duty."

"You're welcome to go do something when I get back." His tone rang of "we've had this conversation before."

Safe for you to say, I thought. *What am I going to go do? I don't want to exercise. I don't have any hobbies. We don't have any money to go shopping. I have no friends who are available at a minute's notice to meet for coffee. They all have kids too. You know I'll just stay here and do nothing.*

"I don't have anything to do," I finally answered.

"Well, don't blame me for that. I'll be back in an hour." He turned toward the door again, but this time completed the task and walked through it and left.

Perhaps it was because I'd been plucked out of my pre-baby life in Portland and dropped in Denver while pregnant that I was so at odds with what to do with myself. I didn't have any earlier life to go back to. It was as if my mom identity started with a clean slate when we moved, and there was no context for the woman who was there before. I spent the next hour flip-flopping between feeling sorry for myself and feeling resentful of Derek.

When he came back, Gabi was awake and I was feeding her in her high chair. He picked her up, his shirt soaked in spots from his sweat, and she started to cry.

"Go," he said, waving his hand toward the door he just walked through. "I've got this."

Gabi reached her arms toward me, her mouth opening wider to let out her screams, as if she understood her father's instructions and wanted to make sure I knew she didn't like the idea. I couldn't leave them like this, with her upset and him annoyed; that wouldn't result in a good outcome, and I wouldn't be relaxed, knowing that's what I was leaving. Besides, where was I going to go?

I reached my arms toward Gabi to rescue her from her Daddy's hold.

"No," Derek said as he pulled her away from me. "You need to go." His voice was firm.

"No." I matched his tone. "It's just easier if I stay." I took Gabi from him, and she immediately stopped crying. Derek and I both looked at each other as if to say, "See? That's exactly what I'm talking about."

In Carol's kitchen, her comment, "Gabi sees you as an extension of herself. Daddy is clearly someone else," rang true. A girl is defined in relation to her parents. Had that been true of me? What did I see when I looked out from my mother's arms? How grateful I was that I had such strong arms holding me, showing me the world. I knew that part of the view was missing, but the landscape she offered was rich.

And then there's that breaking away, a daughter from her mother. Does it ever fully happen if one is the extension of another?

I still see my father when I look in the mirror. His blue eyes and the dark circles underneath. When my nearly black hair is pulled back in a low ponytail, I look like a Spaniard. But these days I am also seeing more of my mother than I ever have. In many ways my life looks markedly different than hers did at my age. But I catch reactions, phrases that sound more like her than ever. Is it because it takes a lifetime for a daughter to separate herself from her mother? Because the bond is tight and makes the breaking away difficult? Impossible? Would I always be this tethered to this child?

It was true, Gabi was happiest when I was holding her and she was facing her daddy. We realized it one day as she was kicking and laughing, facing him. But all that holding was starting to tire me. I felt I was always attached to her physically, or at least with my attention. My sleep schedule, lack of exercise, rare alone time—everything was determined in some way by the baby.

What stops being supportive and becomes unhealthy and consuming? I wondered. Maybe I just needed a hobby. Or an interest. Something to remind me that I was more than a couple of breasts to feed a ten-month-old.

ii

O Christmas Tree

We'd planned this Sunday for months—to drive up to the mountains with a group of friends, Dennis and Jen and Brian and Crystal, to cut down a Christmas tree in the wild. Three families coordinated holiday-packed schedules, Jen purchased date-specific permits from the Forest Service, and we packed thermoses of cocoa and baskets of Christmas cookies to share. A day that would fill Gabi's memory bank for years. Her last Christmas as an only child, now that a new sibling was growing in my belly. A perfect day. And a perfect mama who orchestrated it all.

Our plans changed when Gabi woke up that morning with a fever and then threw up down my shirt.

"If we're going to use the tree permit, you have to go today," I told Derek as I crawled around on her bedroom floor, mopping up the remaining vomit. I was thankful our bedrooms weren't carpeted. "We've already paid for it," I reminded him. The ten-dollar permit had used up our Christmas tree budget.

The year before, we'd bought a house plant at Home Depot and put it on a table so toddler Gabi couldn't spread its dirt all over the floor. I hung a string of lights on the plant and promised myself the next year we'd splurge for a real tree. Memories of U-Cut tree farms surrounding Seattle made me nostalgic for my childhood Christmas traditions, and I jumped at the chance for a scenic drive through the Colorado mountains to bring home a tree in the back of the truck. I could already smell the evergreen that would fill our house with the aroma of Christmas.

In fact, I was gearing up to make Christmas sparkle with tradition. Now that Gabi was old enough to participate, I wanted to make everything around the holiday memorable. I had the sprinkles and cookie cutters ready, the plastic nativity scene unpacked, the Christmas books from the library spread on the coffee table, and, of course, Johnny Mathis playing on the CD player.

My mom did up Christmas with visits to Santa, Christmas ornaments from around the world, and more gifts under the tree than a teacher should have afforded. Her special touches made the holiday feel like a celebration. But after the gifts were open, there was always a little letdown—something, or someone, that I felt was missing. Christmas was one of those things I wanted to get right. I wanted it to be a memory of warmth and security for Gabi. Or was it really for me? To feed into my fantasy of Hallmark living that hadn't been fully realized yet?

If my marriage couldn't fill my empty places and motherhood had more disappointments than I'd expected, I could at least have the Christmas I'd dreamed of. I could control this part of Gabi's childhood.

An hour after Derek left alone to meet up with our friends, I went to the bathroom to relieve my pregnant bladder. I glanced at the shut bathroom door next to me and felt my heart skip: no doorknob! Derek's project the day before was to paint the bedroom and bathroom doors of the main floor of our raised little ranch house. We had a garden-level basement, so our main level was raised half a story above the ground. We figured we could safely leave the house with our high windows open, letting the cool December air in and the paint fumes out while we were gone on our new Christmas tradition. But suddenly I was locked in the bathroom, and my two-year-old was on the other side. I started to sweat as I thought of sick Gabi alone, out of my reach.

"Mommy?" Her voice was softer than usual but was pressed close to the door between us.

"I'll be right out, sweetie. Go lie down." The fading pitter-patter suggested her jammied feet were headed toward her bedroom, and then it was confirmed as Elmo's familiar voice sang out from her book. I pictured her sitting on her bedroom's hardwood floor, the Elmo book open on her lap. Relieved I might have a few minutes to figure out my escape plan, I looked around our tiled purple bathroom.

Then I remembered the open windows throughout the house to let in fresh air! The candles lit in the living room to mask the paint fumes! My heart skipped twice. Elmo stopped singing, and silence followed from behind the door. I quickly ran through the events of the day to assess how I'd gotten to this spot of desperation. Despite my panic, I laughed at the irony of the picturesque day I'd expected.

I looked at the hole in the bathroom door where the doorknob used to be. Of course Derek took off the knobs when he painted the doors the day before. I obviously hadn't thought that through when I pushed the door closed with my foot as I pulled down my pajama pants. I needed to find something that would fit in that hole and turn the latch. I looked around the bathroom again and grabbed my toothbrush from the sink. As I tried to jam it in, the phrase "you can't stick a square peg into a round hole" flashed through my brain. Only, this was a square hole and a round peg.

"Gabi?" I tried not to sound alarmed, but the silence was concerning. No answer. I spun around and opened the medicine cabinet above the sink and grabbed the tweezers. It was a stretch, but maybe they would work. No. My glance flew around the bathroom one more time and landed on the window above the tub. I climbed into the tub, opened the window, and stuck my head out to look down. From window to patio, it was almost a full story. The spigot for the hose was halfway down the wall, and the cement patio spread out below.

"Gabi, I'll be right there. Just stay in your room," I yelled over my shoulder. I wondered if she'd noticed the open window next to her bed. But I was more worried about the candles in the living room that could get knocked over. She'd already blown them out once that day. Why had I cared so much about covering the paint smell?

Climbing up into the window, I wondered if it was worth risking the escape. I could try letting myself down slowly until my foot landed on the spigot, but if that didn't work, I could fall onto the concrete patio. A bigger hazard to the baby I was carrying than some paint fumes. Minutes ticked by as I sat there trying to make my decision to go down or not. I felt truly trapped. I couldn't think of any other options. I peered around the windowsill to my neighbor's yard. Maybe they would hear me if I yelled.

So I started yelling, "Help! I need help!"

How many times before someone heard me?

"Help! I'm stuck!"

I knew my neighbors would come help me figure out how to get out, or if someone parking in front of our house to attend Mass at the church up the street heard, they might call the police. I imagined the police car driving slowly down the alley to find a pregnant woman in the window because she'd locked herself in the bathroom. Martha Stewart probably didn't have a holiday segment on this.

"Hellllp!" After multiple rounds of yelling and no neighbors, I stopped. Still perched on the windowsill, I prayed, *God, help me get to Gabi.* I untangled myself from the window and grabbed my toothbrush again. *Please, please, please,* I prayed as I jammed it in the square hole again. As I turned the toothbrush, I felt the door latch click open and I was free.

I ran into Gabi's bedroom, the location of the last known sound. She was lying facedown, bare chested, her pajamas pulled halfway off. I knelt down next to her and felt the cool hardwood on my feet.

"Gabi?"

Her eyes rolled up toward my voice, telling me it was time for some more Tylenol. I drew her body up and let her legs hang heavy as I draped her around my chest and felt my heart rate slow down.

A few hours later, Derek walked through the front door, holding something with pine needles that looked more like a branch than the full evergreen I was expecting. We wrapped a few of his athletic socks around the trunk so it would be big enough for the Christmas tree stand I'd bought on clearance the previous January.

"They were all kind of like this." I could hear the apology in Derek's voice.

Pathetic was the best descriptor for our tree. Charlie Brown would have been proud.

Later as Gabi napped, I arranged the plastic nativity pieces at the base of the tree and looked over at the boxes of decorations that wouldn't make it out. Our tree was maxed out with the five ornaments already on it, the branches bowing to the floor from their weight. I studied our decorated branch tree with the same single string of lights that had adorned the plant the year before and wondered why nothing seemed to ever live up to expectations.

I rubbed my tummy and remembered the true magic of the first Christmas baby, fully human and fully divine. Such a simple act of becoming one of us, and yet so heavy with the burdens of the world.

As a child, I'd assumed the person missing at the Christmas table was my father. But maybe I was off mark all those years;

maybe it was really Emmanuel. Maybe any holiday meant for a holy remembrance that we forget to remember feels incomplete. I was so busy trying to make the perfect Christmas, I was forgetting to remember Emmanuel, God with us. I took a deep breath and slowly exhaled and remembered.

iii

Daddy's Girls

Genevieve's delivery was similar to Gabi's in many ways. My mom and Derek were there. We were at Rose Hospital in Denver with the same ob-gyn and the same labor and delivery nurse. But in many ways it was different: easier, more natural. Derek and I laughed with the doctor between pushes, and when girl number two arrived, she looked familiar because she looked like her sister. Derek and I made a certain combination, and Genevieve had the look. I didn't know her yet, but I would. And I knew the kind of consuming love that was ahead. My heart and arms were familiar with mothering.

Derek spent every free minute of Gabi's first years of life remodeling our fixer house. Painting, putting in sinks, repairing floorboards. I cared for the baby. We split our duties in a traditional domestic way. He went to work. I did laundry. He made house repairs. I made dinner. For the most part we were happy with that arrangement.

When Genevieve arrived, the old way of doing things didn't work as well. Derek took Gabi when I couldn't. No longer the center of my universe, child number one studied me holding her new baby sister—she was now in Daddy's arms watching Mommy. The dynamic in the house had shifted. And we all had to figure out how it was going to work.

"Where's Daddy?" nearly three-year-old Gabi asked as she walked in the kitchen. Her baby sister had been home for a few weeks, and Gabi had been spending more time than ever with Dad. It was a Saturday, so although her routines looked similar to the rest of the week, there was an added difference—Daddy was around.

"I don't know." The harsh tone of my voice surprised even me. I was too tired to care. She was right. Where *was* he? "I think he's in the garage," I answered.

"Is he making something?" she asked, indicating she knew her daddy's handyman habits all too well.

"A coffee table, I think."

I watched Gabi walk to the kitchen door and stand on her tiptoes to reach the brass doorknob for the security door that led outside. She pushed it open and disappeared into the backyard and beyond in search of Daddy.

Like with marriage, I didn't have a picture of what my husband's parenting would look like. As we adjusted our roles to life with kids, I had a blank slate to draw from. I knew what I didn't want. I didn't want him to be absent. And Derek was present, faithfully going to work every day to a job that felt on the stifling side so he could provide for us, his girls. There was no question he was present and accounted for, what I wanted in my daughters' father. So why was I so frequently annoyed?

I checked on the baby still asleep in the bassinet and followed Gabi through the kitchen door. Stepping onto the back porch, I could hear the radio blaring from the garage, the announcer's voice giving his monotone report on the Colorado Rockies baseball game. The high-pitched squeal of the table saw interrupted the announcer's commentary, confirming Derek was indeed making something. I scanned the backyard, looking for Gabi. The deck. The king-sized sandbox Derek made as Gabi's first-year birthday gift. The swing in the back corner he'd hung from the high tree branch for her. The slide he picked up on the side of the road and brought home like a warrior with bounty for his princess.

I followed the noise into the garage. Derek had pulled the cars out in order to make room for his table saw. And there next to him was his companion in construction, riding her red tricycle around the random obstacle course of scrap lumber on the concrete floor.

They simultaneously looked up at me as I stepped in the doorway, and they smiled. A happy pair doing their thing.

"Can she reach that blade?" I asked as I assessed the height of the table saw and the reach of Gabi's arm.

"No," he answered without looking at it.

"Are there any nails in those pieces of wood?" My eyes fell on the scrap pieces spread around the floor. I glanced around the garage for other potential hazards. I was worried he wasn't going to do what he needed to in order to protect her. That she wouldn't be safe. That he wouldn't do things the way I would do them.

And there was the crux of my angst. I wanted him to do things like me when he wasn't meant to. Gabi had two capable parents, but I wasn't giving Derek the freedom to parent his way. To be her father. His was a side-by-side, relaxed approach. A big-picture approach. I often got stressed about lunch dishes getting washed or leaving the house on time. The immediate tasks of the moment that needed to get done. And if I was stressed about them, I thought everyone should be. I became angry, resentful, when he didn't find the same urgency in getting the diaper changed.

"Mommy, look at Daddy's toffee table!" Gabi exclaimed.

Derek pushed his safety goggles from his eyes up to his forehead. I silently admitted that if he was following his eighth-grade shop class rules for eye protection, he would certainly have the forethought to protect his daughter from the tools.

"Well, what do you think?" he asked as he tilted a piece of wood up for me to see. He motioned to the corner of the garage, and I saw what looked like the metal base of a coffee table.

"I found it in the dumpster," he said of the orphaned base. "I'll just spray paint it and we'll have a new table."

I had unknowingly married an artist. A dumpster-diving, tool-wielding artist whose studio was his workshop. I knew deep in the caverns of my brain that whispers of the past were present, pushing on my subconscious to resent his weekend warrior activities in the garage. *Where is he?* they would whisper. *He's leaving you, his girls, while he's off being creative, alone.* But I also knew those pushes, those messages, weren't true. He'd rather have us join him, listening to the Rockies game and playing on the tricycle, than not. But he also needed that outlet to unwind from the stresses of providing for his family.

I turned to go back in the house to be within earshot of the baby. The truth was that his laid-back approach, his relaxed nature, was part of what I fell in love with years earlier. I wasn't afraid he would explode at the littlest thing, and he offered wise, big-picture perspective. We were both growing into our constantly shifting roles. As I was learning to let go of some of my expectations about mothering, I was learning I needed to give him freedom to be the father he uniquely was. Formed out of the man he uniquely was. I needed to appreciate he was present. With his safety goggles on.

iv

Retreat

The MOPS group at Corona Presbyterian became my sisterhood. The women I called on for last-minute babysitting, went out with for a rare dinner without families, and laughed with until Diet Coke came out my nose. I was following Julie's lead to trust in grace and let others do the same. Julie was stepping down as the group's coordinator. She needed someone to take over, and I agreed to help.

I sat on the stone hearth in front of the fireplace, the cool seeping through my pajama pants onto my outstretched legs. I felt like I was home in lots of ways. The women with me were my closest mothering friends. Some, like Cindy and Kathy, I'd met through the group, and others, like Jen and Crystal and Kristi, I'd recruited to join. We were on a summer retreat at my in-laws' house, a half hour outside of Denver, but it may as well have been Mexico with the vacation-like quality of a night away from kids. We were planning the year ahead for the group of fifty or so moms we knew as our MOPS group. The living room was obviously familiar to me, my weekly getaway spot where Derek and the girls and I often got together with extended family for long weekend dinners. Sitting there, with it filled with the friends I'd prayed for those first months of motherhood, I felt God's provision in their presence.

Earlier that day, when everyone arrived and saw their personalized clipboards and notebooks out waiting for them, Kathy turned to me. "How do you do it? You always have everything so together." I thought of the hours put in to making goody bags, photocopying agendas, and planning meals. That performance side of me wanted to do it right for appearance's sake. To show that I was capable, in control, put together. I was willing to get the details just so at the expense of my stress level. Derek did not have the pleasure of a peaceful wife the week leading up to the retreat.

"Oh, it's nothing," I said as I waved my hand at the table decorations, but Kathy's comment gave me just what I was wanting: affirmation. Affirmation that I was good at other things besides doing dishes and wiping bottoms. I'd done plenty of other things in my pre-mothering days, but the last few years I'd been consumed with laundry and running errands to Home Depot. That year I'd sat on a committee for some changes at our local elementary school, but leading this MOPS group was my first time leading a team. Ever.

I put my glass down on the hearth and leaned in. We'd been doing a team-building exercise all day, taking turns telling our life stories. Hours earlier, we'd each taken a poster board and some markers and spread around the house for twenty minutes of alone time to make a life map of significant events in our lives. A visual of where we'd been and how that shaped who we'd become. Some showed topography with high and low elevation changes, others a winding path with stops along the way. Mine was the earth with lines showing a mess of back-and-forth stops between Europe and the United States, to Colorado and Portland and Colorado again.

The plan was that we'd each take fifteen minutes to share our stories between planning sessions. But how does one sum up her life in fifteen minutes? One person's fifteen minutes bled into an hour.

So there we were after dinner, pajama clad, settling in for more stories.

"Pass her the Kleenex," I whispered to Crystal, who was sitting next to Kathy.

It was inevitable with each one that the tears would start flowing. Going back to places in memory where we hadn't been in years. Realizing how it was impacting us today. We said things like:

"I didn't realize how close to the surface this was."

"I haven't thought about that in years."

"I don't want my kids to have to go through that too."

And that's when it struck me: we were all talking about pains from somewhere in our childhood. They must be an inevitable part of life, of parenting, that hurt—those valleys, those low points, are unavoidable. The realization that I wasn't alone felt hopeful. Being raised by imperfect people is a universal experience. And seeing how we all had grown as a result of those painful experiences made me appreciate them in a new way. Many of my good qualities stemmed from things that were difficult in the moment.

"We better start saving for our kids' therapy now," I said, "because they'll certainly be blaming us for something when they're our age."

My short fuse the day before flashed in my mind.

"Gabi, put these things away," I'd snapped as I threw toys into their baskets in her room.

She stood frozen, staring at me.

"Come on. Move!" Was English not her first language? Did she not see I was trying to clean up?

The snapping came with more intensity and faster than I would have liked. And it was frequently my reaction. *Maybe she won't remember,* I thought. *She's still only four.* But I knew that wasn't the point. I wanted to raise her in an environment of love, and instead I was getting stressed about toys on the floor and acting like the mess was a personal attack. But if it was true that my imperfection as a mother was inevitable, how did I balance what I wanted with what I could realistically offer?

Any confidence I'd had from pulling the details of the day together was now shadowed by the guilt of falling short with my kids.

I looked around the room at the others in my grown-up slumber party. Makeup cried off, hair pulled back in sloppy buns, most barefoot, and some even pregnant.

"How do we do this?" I asked. What "this" was, I wasn't completely sure. This life with its topography of ups and downs. How do we manage to keep pressing forward, dragging our baggage behind us? How do we help each other through it? How do we mother, knowing we will make mistakes? Mistakes that would certainly impact our kids?

Kathy wiped her wet cheeks with a tissue, looked at me, and waited for me to answer my own question.

"I don't know," she finally said. "Pray, I guess. Isn't Jesus always the right answer in Sunday school?"

I didn't know either, but I supposed she was right. I was a mess. Despite my efforts to be slow to anger, I was falling short all over the place. All I could do was pray. For patience. For grace. To remember grace had already been extended by the grace giver. He was the right answer. The best I could do was expect my own imperfection, offer grace to others, and hope they would do the same for me.

Section 8

The Main Thing

i

Anger

I've had a headache for eight days." Derek rubbed his temples as he said it. "I'm sure it's a brain tumor. I've been waiting to find out when it would be my turn. I'm genetically predisposed," he added, referring to his dad's recent diagnosis of brain cancer. Our life with cancer was causing us to make wildly morbid, inappropriate jokes with increasing frequency.

"Ha-ha" was my sarcastic response.

"No, I'm serious. I think I have a brain tumor."

Examining his face, I couldn't see any break of a smirk, and I realized he was serious. He'd convinced himself there was something wrong.

"It's stress related," the doctor told Derek when he went in. Not a surprise, since both of his parents had recently been diagnosed with advanced stages of cancer and were undergoing treatment. And Derek was daily going to a job that felt like prison, sitting at a desk and watching the clock as he wondered if this was what the rest of life held. Hospitals. Cubicles. And bills.

"So what are you going to do about it?" I asked Derek when he relayed the doctor's diagnosis. I was tired. Worn down. Exhausted from the emotional ups and downs of the last cancer-filled year. Emergency hospital visits. Days in waiting rooms with two kids. Hopeful news and then devastating setbacks.

And my husband with his ever-increasing headaches. He couldn't sleep. He was retreating into himself. Not talking. Not sharing. A wall was slowly building up, invisible brick by invisible brick, between us.

The truth was he had shared in the past and I didn't respond well. His job was feeling like a slow death. Every day he went to an office and stared at the walls and his clock, watching the minutes and the hours tick away.

"I need something more than this," he said.

"We have more. We have kids. We have our life." Why couldn't he see that sometimes a job is a means to an end? Why couldn't he see that now was the time to enjoy life, to be happy? From the outside, we were living the life I'd always wanted, and he was ruining it. Yes, I thought that. I thought his poor attitude was ruining everything.

"Looking ahead at my life, I thought I'd love my job. Like when we were at the Dale House. It was hard, but I knew I counted for something. Now I feel replaceable. But maybe that's what grown-up life is. Maybe this is real life, and we just didn't know it when we were younger."

"Sometimes life doesn't work out the way we want," I snapped back. "Our response is what matters."

Even as I said those words, I knew I wasn't good at putting them into practice. As far back as I can remember, I knew this lesson, but I still wanted life on my terms. Life doesn't always look like you think it should. Sometimes life isn't fair. As a girl, I hated when my mom told me that. Probably because it smelled of so much truth. Prayers don't always get answered the way we want. Dads don't call. So we have a choice: to move forward and enjoy God's blessings that are in our midst, or sulk. Why didn't he see that?

"It's different for men," he said. "Our jobs are tied up in our identities differently. In a way, I am what I do."

I got it. Kind of. I got it in a way that I didn't feel it but could imagine what he was saying. But I was still mad. Angry that he couldn't just snap out of it.

I was finding anger was too often my first response.

Six months earlier, my mothering accomplice Jen called to tell me some news. "I'm going to take a temp job as a social worker." The lilt in her voice indicated she was excited.

I was confused. Why would she want to go back to work?

"I've been so restless, like I haven't been using all of myself, and I want to see if going back to work is what's missing."

What's missing? Using all of yourself? Isn't part of motherhood dying to self? I could feel myself judging all over the place, but I didn't care. Going back to work was not what we did, and I felt strangely betrayed. It's not like we'd made a pact of any kind or even said these things out loud. Still, I felt abandoned.

"I'll have to work on Fridays, so I'll miss the last three MOPS meetings, but I'll get the door covered," she said, referring to her role as official greeter in the group.

Now it felt legitimately personal, like she was letting me down. She wasn't following through on her responsibilities. On what she promised me she'd do. I had no awareness that the reason it felt so personal was because it was tapping into all of my childhood issues of desertion. Poor Jen didn't either. She just wanted to go back to work.

In the weeks that followed, Jen called on her days off. "It's fun. I've missed this, but I miss you," she reported.

If you weren't working, you'd see me, I thought. I missed her too, but I couldn't see past my own disappointment to celebrate with my friend. I let my hurt and newfound insecurity stand in the way. I was still holding on to the idea that there was a right way to mother, and the biggest factor in the way I'd done things up to that point was to stay at home full-time. She was challenging that notion. Implying she might be a better mom if she went back to work. That there was more than one right way.

Spring turned into summer, which turned into fall. The phone rang as I carried my empty suitcases up from the basement.

"I don't know why you're treating me this way." Jen's familiar voice sounded garbled on the other end of the line.

Standing in my living room, I got the feeling this was going to be a long conversation.

"I feel like you're making fun of me in front of everyone."

I was shocked and a little bit annoyed. What was she talking about? I did a quick mental inventory of the last few weeks and all of the places we'd been together. I thought of our last MOPS meeting and remembered making a quick joke from the stage about Jen, but I thought it was in fun.

"I can't go on the trip with you if you're going to keep treating me this way."

I felt it was safe to roll my eyes since she couldn't see me. We were getting ready to leave in a few days for the MOPS Convention, and I had a thousand things to do to get ready. Gabi was at preschool and Genevieve was taking a nap; this was precious productive time. I didn't want to use it talking to Jen about her hurt feelings.

"Well, I'm sorry." I could hear the snap in my voice. I tried to take a deep breath and not feel so defensive. Part of me knew she was right, but the other part wanted to explain it away. I was busy, rushed. I thought we were just playing around. I wasn't being literal when I made comments.

But I knew it was the pent-up frustration of the spring and summer bubbling up in side comments. The feelings of anger, betrayal, insecurity, and then embarrassment that had snowballed into one big not-such-a-good-friend mess. And the snippy side comments that came out were clothed as jokes but really were intended to hurt, with a bite that she could detect and I didn't want to own up to.

My pastor, Steve, tells us that the main thing is to keep the main thing the main thing. And when Jesus was asked if he had to pick one thing for us to do, one rule to follow, what it would be, he answered to love God with our everything and to love those around us like we wanted to be loved. I certainly wasn't following those instructions.

Jen and I talked for an hour. I could hear the hurt in her voice from my comments the week before, and I was truly sorry. I didn't know why my snippiness was seeping out all over the place. With my kids. With Derek. With her. In all my attempts to live the right way, I wasn't doing what God called me most to do: to love the people around me.

ii

Change

As far as I'm concerned, she gets a pass on everything." Derek had just hung up the phone with his mom. She was canceling plans to come down to Denver for dinner and wanted to know if we would make the half-hour commute up to her house instead. She'd been changing plans a lot lately, which often meant us schlepping kids a half hour each way, no adherence to bedtime, and late-night car rides home filled with exhausted screaming from the backseat. Changes that would have annoyed me in the past. But Derek was right. She should get a pass. She was on chemotherapy, and so was Derek's dad. They were living a double cancer life, and they deserved to act like pure lunatics if they wanted to.

I knew my big-picture husband was wise, so I decided to follow his lead. Give a pass. Comments she made that in the past I would have resented: I gave a pass. Plans changed that were an inconvenience: I gave a pass. It was easier to let things slide when she was so sick. I couldn't fault her for not wanting to make the half-hour drive. And there was the possibility these were our last days with her. Her prognosis was not good. Would this be the last birthday she would celebrate for this grandchild? The last Thanksgiving she would be at the table?

As I made the conscious decision to let things go, I noticed my attitude started shifting. I remembered past comments and how internally I'd stewed, and realized how often I simply chose to take my mother-in-law's words the wrong way. Give a pass. I was doing a better job of keeping the main thing the main thing.

It was easy to be gentle with a grandmother dying of cancer. It was not so easy with a husband who seemed fully capable. Capable to meet my needs. I was angry that he wasn't able to snap out of his funk. And because of my anger, the invisible wall grew thicker, taller. A barrier between us. I couldn't go to him with my daily hurts or with my isolation because he was the reason for my isolation. Well, the wall was.

A silence developed. My confidant, the person I dreamed with, was slipping away, emotionally unavailable. Gone were the late-night talks, the whispers of love, the confessions of hurt. We spoke about life's logistics, but real-life matters, those of the heart, were off-limits. I didn't want to hear that he was unhappy, and he knew that, so he didn't want to talk about it.

The nights were the worst. Lying in bed, I'd hear his steady breathing indicating he was asleep. And I'd wonder if this was it. Maybe Derek's fears were justified; maybe this was as good as life got. Two kids I adored. A husband who seemed distant. In-laws who were sick. God never promised me life would be easy, but where was the joy? I couldn't become one of those women who got her needs met through her children. But I was starting to understand how that could happen.

So I prayed. Prayed like I'd never prayed before—out of loneliness. *God, please fix us. Fix him. Fix me.*

In time I heard the shallowness of those prayers. They implied we'd get to a point where we'd arrived, and I knew that was impossible this side of heaven. We were works in progress until then.

The prayers evolved to *God, change us*. Things weren't working, so something had to change, and it seemed like it should be us. God was consistent, never changing. He wasn't the problem, so we must have been. But I knew that implied that when Derek changed, then I would be content. That it was about him.

The prayer finally became *God, change me.* Oh, that honest self-examination can be painful. Harsh. I knew God wanted me. My heart. And he didn't want it anger-soaked. Dipped and saturated with resentment. And I knew I couldn't change on my own. I'd tried and I'd failed. *God, change me. Help me to love him better. To not be so selfish. Change my heart.*

The nightly prayers as I heard the breathing next to me spilled over into morning prayers as I made my coffee. Scooping the grounds into the filter, I prayed, *Lord, change me. I'm starting this day with a terrible attitude. Change me.*

Gabi would cling to me as I dropped her off at preschool. I was annoyed, wanting to maximize my two hours of errand running without a three-year-old, and she wouldn't let me leave. *Lord, help me to remember I'm the adult in this relationship. Help my patience right now. Change me.*

The "change me" prayers began to seep into other areas. As I looked at our bank account on the computer screen, the pending bills more than the amount available, I prayed, *Lord, change me. Help me to trust that this will work out. Help me to trust that you will provide.* I kept praying because I saw it was making a difference. I felt better when I sent up those silent prayers. I was involving God in my every struggle. Not to change the circumstances but to change my heart.

After a while I could look back and see my prayers were being answered. He was changing me. It was true my anger was melting. I wasn't so quick to snap. But it was more than that. I was realizing my actions weren't defining me; my anchoring in the grace giver was.

The fruit of the Spirit—love, patience, self-control—we'd spent a whole year at MOPS learning about it. Before that, I didn't know these qualities were more accessible, more evident the closer you were to their source. So I went to the source with more frequency. *God, change me.*

Months later we found out Derek's disposition was more than just a bad mood. It was chemical—he was clinically depressed. Once he was treated, I felt I had my old husband back. His spark and his humor returned.

But he wasn't returning to the same wife. I'd changed. Before I got to that place of change, I'd had to walk through some dark months. Dark for me. Dark for us. Had I not felt so angry, so alone, I wouldn't have gone to the source of love as consistently, as desperately, as I did. But when I finally did, his grace was waiting and took me in and changed me.

iii

The Right Way

I stared at the dirty dishes in the sink and thought about how much I hated them. The caked-on tomato sauce revealed they'd been sitting there since lunchtime. I needed to tackle them. Derek would be home soon, and I didn't want to admit that another day went by and I'd managed to avoid my chores. I was mastering the skill of stepping over piles of toys to get to those tasks that energized me: making phone calls and sending emails for our MOPS group.

I loved everything about my job as the coordinator. The meetings. The creativity. The energy of being part of something with a larger purpose, bringing moms into the fold to tell them they had a place where they were welcome. Where they could be encouraged. Checklists were created and completed. Tasks were delegated and events produced. I loved my girls and being their mother, but I had to admit these other tasks were fueling me in a different way. I was gravitating toward wanting more of it in my days. In fact, as I prayed, *God, change me,* I was feeling his pull toward other things.

I'd never been a good housekeeper. I could discipline myself to clean the toilets, but my heart didn't sing when the laundry got done or things were in order. I had friends, Jen included, who found great satisfaction in spending the day organizing closets. And yet, even she needed a break from the housework. Work offered that for her.

The truth was Jen's decision to go back to work had impacted my own thoughts on the subject. Despite my resentment of her changing her mind, it opened a door to options I'd never been willing to walk through before. Could that really be a possibility for me too? I dared not say it aloud. It would require admitting there wasn't a right way.

As I found my heart changed, I began to trust God with more. If he could take my anger and soften it, he could certainly be trusted with other parts of my life. My marriage. My children. Even my talents. Maybe my ideas about motherhood, my priorities, and what I was called to do with each day were totally off. Maybe I was placing my prescription for motherhood above all else and giving it a disproportionate amount of weight in defining myself and my life.

I wanted God to change all of me, so maybe . . . probably . . . I needed to trust God with all of me.

"Gabi! Stop it!" I grabbed the marker cap and jammed it back on. We sat at the dining room table together while Genevieve napped in their bedroom. Gabi was using the front of my magazine as a coloring page, despite my instructions thirty seconds earlier not to. My eyes went back to the bank statement in my hand. Another month, and I wasn't sure how our bills were going to get paid. They always did, but the savings account didn't leave much space for going over budget.

We could use more money, and I wasn't winning any mothering awards. The blissful stay-at-home mom I was not. Four years of living paycheck to paycheck, and I was drained from the daily stress about the budget. I was getting to the point where the thought of figuring out child care sounded less stressful than facing another month of bills I couldn't pay. All of the moms I'd judged in years past for making a healthy, or just plain necessary, decision for themselves and their families flooded to the front of my mind. I wanted to crawl under my bed in embarrassment.

"I think I might want to go back to work," I finally had the courage to tell Derek out loud. The internal seed had sprouted weeks earlier, but the guilt was there. I felt I couldn't leave my girls, so I didn't say anything. But I had started looking for jobs online, picturing what life as a working mom might look like. I knew I had to tell him.

He raised his eyebrows. "Okaaay." He drew out the word, knowing there was so much in there. He'd always said I could decide how much or little I worked outside the home, and he stood by that, but there were lots of logistical questions. What about child care? Schedule? What would I do?

"I don't know," I said, "but I feel like it's time to at least explore it."

"Okay." He paused, and I could tell those logistical questions were swirling around in his brain like they had been in mine the last few weeks. "We aren't the first family to figure this out." He put his arms around me. It was going to be okay. We had no other option but to trust that.

"I just don't know what I'll do about child care," I told my sister-in-law Lindsay. She had recently moved with her family from California to Colorado after her parents' cancer diagnosis. "It's so expensive. It almost doesn't make working worth it. Besides, I can't leave them just anywhere."

My heart felt torn. I was starting to believe God was directing me this way. Prompting me to get out of the house, to admit I wasn't a domestic diva and my kids would benefit from a thriving mom.

But I couldn't get past this hurdle of leaving them with someone else. Even if it was for only a few days a week.

"I'll watch them for you," Lindsay said. "If it's just a couple of days a week, I'll watch them until you figure something out."

I knew what it was like to watch other people's kids for an entire day. That was no small offer. But her voice didn't reflect the gloom I would have felt if I was saying those words. I wanted to scream, "Yes!" but I didn't know how I could accept such generosity, so I didn't say anything.

"We moved here for Karis to be with her cousins," Lindsay answered my silence. "Besides, that's what family does."

It hung there—"that's what family does"—between us. I knew that. I'd had that with my mom and my aunt. My cousin and I were always being cared for by the other's mom. We were one big mushy group. And Lindsay's comment connected us that way. Sisters of sorts. I would never have the childhood memories she shared with Derek or Kendall, but she was offering a generous gift of her time and energy. Because we were family.

So my girls were taken care of. Now I just needed to come to grips with the shift in my perspective. Or, really, with what I was sensing from the Holy Spirit, that mysterious third part of God in three persons who nudges our hearts, speaks to us in hints and whispers, and every once in a while shouts. I felt God saying, "Follow me. Follow me with your talents. With your days. If you are under my wings, following my call, you are mothering the right way." And a weight was lifted. I couldn't identify it until it was gone. But there was a new freedom. Slowly I was starting to get it.

My purpose was to follow God in every area of my life. I was learning to keep the main thing the main thing.

Section 9

The Accident

i

Headlines

Derek sat at the table with the newspaper open as I topped off his coffee like a diner waitress. We'd been on the verge of an argument all morning. Biting comments back and forth that hinted at the regular annoyances. Me thinking he was awfully sedentary for a man who was about to leave me alone with two kids on a Saturday. Him thinking he would like to enjoy a cup of coffee in peace before going to a day of church meetings. Despite the thought of hours of two whiny kids and housework ahead, I was partly grateful he was leaving so we could stop the bickering. We were all going to Kristi and Jeff's for dinner that night; I would have some social element to the day that I could look forward to.

Derek put his coffee cup down on the table with a definitive clunk.

"Look at this." He pointed to an article on the second page of the paper. I looked down at a headline that read "Two children killed in hit and run." Above the article was a picture of a mangled stroller on a dark downtown Denver street, with a police car in the background.

"It happened last night." He read me the first paragraph. A family—mother, father, girl, and boy—were crossing an intersection downtown when they were plowed down by a pickup that sped through a red light. The truck and driver were still at large. Witnesses say the mom was pushing the kids in a double stroller and the kids both died on the scene. Denver police reported the mother was in critical condition. It sounded like the father had survived.

My mind did a two-second inventory of our friends we would see later that night, all with a girl and a boy: Jen and Dennis, Crystal and Brian, Kristi and Jeff. Any of those families could easily have been out for an evening stroll downtown. *But what are the chances it was one of them?* I thought. *Unlikely,* I just as quickly concluded. I wondered who this mystery family was and if I had any connection to them. Denver was a big city with a three-degrees-of-separation reputation.

Derek focused his gaze on the picture and shook his head back and forth as if telling the newspaper, "No, this isn't possible." His eyes moved up to my face where I stood, the coffeepot perched in my hand. His expression silently asked, "Why do we fight so much?" I knew he was thinking that could have been us.

I took a deep breath and exhaled slowly. He was a good husband. I should be grateful he was spending the day ahead offering his skills to our church. I placed my hand on his shoulder and let it linger a few seconds before I turned to walk back into the kitchen. A silent apology of sorts.

A few hours later, the phone rang. Still working on getting the breakfast dishes finished, I wiped my soapy hands on my shirt and picked up the phone. "Hello?"

"Did you see the news?!"

I could tell it was Jen, but she sounded garbled. Was she crying?

"Did you see the news?!" she shot out again.

"What? Is everything okay?"

Gabi and Genevieve were playing in the living room only feet away, and recognizing I was on the phone, they instinctively raised their voices three octaves.

"The accident. Did you see the news about the accident?" Now I could tell she was crying. I could barely understand her words.

"What? What accident?"

"The accident downtown."

My mind flashed to the picture in the paper. I couldn't breathe. Was it Crystal? Kristi?

The girls were starting to scream in the next room. I couldn't hear, I couldn't understand, but I knew something was very wrong. I pressed the phone as close to my ear as it would allow and plugged my other ear with my finger as I ran down the steps into the basement to get away from the kid noise.

"Yes. Yes, the accident downtown. I heard about it," I answered quickly. I tried to swallow and braced myself for what her next words were going to be.

"It was Becca. We think she died."

A flash of relief flew through me. Who was Becca? I didn't know who Jen was talking about. She knew everyone, and though we went many places together, she must be confused. She was talking about someone I'd never met.

"Who's Becca?" I shouted into the phone

The screaming from upstairs was following me down. I went into our guest bedroom and closed the door.

"Who is Becca?" I yelled again.

"Becca Bingham. She was at MOPS last Friday."

The MOPS reference made me freeze. I must know her. This was my group. But my mind was blank. I couldn't picture her. How did I not know who she was? I thought I knew everyone in our group.

Jen continued. "We think she died. Cindy called me. She heard it from friends from their old church this morning."

This was not making sense. I didn't know who this Becca was, and there seemed to be lots of holes in the information.

Jen couldn't talk. Through her sobs I made out, "I'll call you back." And *click*, she hung up.

I sat frozen on the bed, my hand grasping the phone inches away from my ear. I wanted to understand what she'd said, and at the same time I didn't. That inner conflict made even holding the phone confusing. I needed to figure out what was going on. I needed to *do* something. To control the situation. How could I find out? How could this be true? What was I supposed to do? I was in charge of this group of moms, or at least that's what our group structure said. That's why Jen called me.

I needed someone to tell me what to do. I thought of Carol. She'd be home on a Saturday morning. She'd know what I should do.

When I heard her "Hello?" I tried to swallow. It was now my turn to be the hysterical caller on the line. My breaths came out in choppy spurts, garbling my words as I pushed them out. "Accident. Kids killed. Mom from my MOPS group." Somehow I was able to describe an outline of what I knew to be happening.

"Oh, Alex!"

Those two words were just what I needed—someone to confirm that this was horrific.

"Okay, let me see if I can find anything."

Thank God. She was going to take over. To tell me what I should do. I could hear the clicking of the keys on her computer keyboard.

"Here it is. On the *Denver Post* site." Then silence as I assumed she was reading.

She quickly read me the first few sentences out loud. The accident. Hit-and-run. Two children. A boy and a girl. Killed. I knew all that. I wanted her to get to new information. Who was the mom?

"It is just confirmed the mother has died at Denver Health Medical Center." Carol stopped and then said again, "Oh, Alex!"

I couldn't breathe.

ii

GRIEF

Jen called back. She'd confirmed through trails of mutual friends that it was Becca Bingham. And I had confirmed she had died. My heart broke wide open, tore open as if being ripped from my chest, at the thought of one of our own being killed on the street. Jen, who really did know everyone, started filling me in on Becca's details. Becca had only come to MOPS a handful of times that fall. She brought two-year-old Garrison with her. But her four-year-old daughter, Macie, was in preschool on Friday mornings. Becca was friends with Cindy. They were nurses at the Children's Hospital together. They had gone to the same church years earlier. Cindy ran into her at the pool over the summer and invited her to MOPS. I was starting to remember there were emails over the summer. She'd asked about coming and I'd replied. But why couldn't I recall her face?

I quickly shifted into action mode. I wanted to do something. Plan something. Fix this. Make things right. Make it better. I thought of the moms in our group. I wanted to protect them somehow. The grief. The fear. She was one of us. If it could happen to her, it could happen to anyone. Questions that would come up. Jen and I made a plan for a phone tree; it was better for moms to hear from each other than to see the story on the news. We had no idea what the next few hours or days would hold, but having a plan would make us feel better, like we could control something.

"I love you," Jen said as she hung up. It was the beginning of saying things we didn't want to go unsaid.

As I hung up, the sobs came out. *Oh, God, why? Why did this have to happen? Why would you let this happen? Hold me up, Lord, because I'm already falling. Collapsing. God, where are you?*

I walked upstairs to the kitchen and called the church. I needed my husband home.

That night our family of four packed into the minivan and went to Kristi and Jeff's for dinner as planned, but everything was different. I walked in their house from the dark November night to the smell of Kristi's chili percolating on the stove. There were candles lit on their dining room table, and from the front door I could see into the kitchen and hear familiar voices. The tears turned on again. I was uncontrollably grateful for a warm house, friends who understood, and my husband and children safely with me.

Walking into the kitchen, I greeted each friend with a hug. A gripping, clinging embrace that lasted longer than my usual half pat on the back. I didn't want to let go. Of anyone. It felt as though God had turned the world upside down like a salt shaker and shaken it up, leaving some things as they'd been only hours earlier and letting other things, like the sense of security in crossing the street, fall out and disappear forever.

Later that night, I sat on the edge of Gabi's toddler bed and picked up my sleeping girl. I draped her body across mine and felt the weight and warmth of it press down on me. Her breathing, in and out, in and out, seemed so miraculous. So precious. I sat in the dark with the light from the hall spilling on the floor near my feet, held my daughter in my arms, and cried for what felt like the thousandth time that day. I prayed, *God, please. Please don't separate me from my babies. Ever.*

The next week was a blur of tears. Our church held a prayer service for our moms and the community. Every cover of the *Denver Post* that week was splashed with pictures of Becca and Macie and Garrison. Giving daily updates of apprehending the suspects. Retracing their bar-hopping night and the miracle of the dropped license plate at the scene of the accident. Showing photos of strangers placing flowers at the downtown intersection. Giving descriptions of the princess and Superman Halloween costumes worn by the kids as they sat in the double stroller. And quotes from Becca's neighbors about her sweet nature and her reputation for rescuing stray animals.

Denver was caught in communal grief as everyone placed themselves in the scene. *What if that was my wife? My kids? Me, crossing that street?* As a result, any detail that could be discovered by the media was. It was impossible to escape the story. Turn on the television, walk into the coffee shop, and their three faces were there. And I felt like I was in the eye of the storm. That I had a personal connection to her. That she was one of us. One of this group that I led.

I sat at a funeral of hundreds surrounded by a dozen women from my MOPS group and watched three caskets carried down the center aisle to the front of the church. One big one and two little ones. A princess cape draped over one and a Superman cape over another. Followed by a man with hunched shoulders and his arm in a sling. The closest he would get to walking his daughter down the aisle.

Every thought about Becca's husband became a thought about Derek. Picturing him suddenly alone in the world. The unimaginable had become real in front of me. Her funeral could just as easily have been my funeral. Why was I spared yesterday, today, and she wasn't? There was a disconnect between how I thought

God should work and sitting at this funeral, watching a home video of two-year-old Garrison following his dad around the yard with a toy lawn mower.

I canceled our MOPS speaker for the next week and had a counselor, a friend of Carol's, come in to lead our first meeting after the accident. We passed the microphone around our group, giving everyone a chance to share, with permission to say and feel anything. Some moms remembered Becca's last time at MOPS only two weeks earlier. How she talked about what she was planning to buy her kids for Christmas, the red shoes she wore, her new haircut. Many in her discussion group remembered the craft collage she'd made a few meetings earlier. Pictures cut out of magazines and glued onto a sheet of paper as a self-depiction of who she was. At the center of the collage, she'd drawn a cross, "because Jesus is the center of my life," she'd said.

"She was so peaceful when she said it," a mom from her group commented, "and so confident." We all wondered what that meant about where she was now, only weeks later.

The counselor suggested we find a project we could work on together as a way to collectively process Becca's death. Remembering how her husband asked that children's books be donated at the funeral, we offered to organize the books. A few awkward phone calls with Becca's husband, Frank, and we found ourselves sorting through boxes of books in a basement storage room in a Denver elementary school, organizing thousands of books by grade-reading levels. Every time I talked to Frank, I forced back the tears and felt guilty that my grief might be making more work for him. The last thing I wanted was to burden him with a bunch of weepy women he'd never met. And yet I wanted to convey that our hearts were breaking alongside his.

In twos and threes we worked. Getting to know each other and processing unexpected circumstances and grief. We prayed for the kids who would receive and read the books. Prayed for ourselves and for Frank. It was a tangible action that allowed us to be together. To know we weren't alone.

Outside of our MOPS group, people didn't always get it. My jaw dropped as she said it—another mom making a flippant comment with an unintended sting: "I don't know why you're so upset. You didn't even know her."

A slap in the face. A judgment of my emotional reaction to the whole thing.

This other mom who wasn't part of our MOPS group looked at me and asked, "Why are you crying about this again?" Her question hurt, and I resolved she obviously didn't get the importance of this group. How precious each woman was.

Though I felt defensive, even weeks later I couldn't shake her question. Why *was* I so upset? She was right, I hadn't known Becca. Why was this shaking me to my core?

iii

THE WALL

As I write this five years later, I think about the question of why Becca's death shook me so deeply. I'm surprised that even now I grieve this woman I didn't know. My pastor, Steve Garcia, spoke at my new MOPS group recently. A different group than the one Becca had been part of. One that I felt compelled to help start because of the growth I experienced through her loss. One of those unexpected places where the ripples of her death are still felt.

We asked Steve to speak on the spiritual development of kids and how we as moms influence our children. Perched on a stool in his shorts and KEEN shoes, he was right to start the morning by saying, "We can apply these principles to our kids, but really this information is for us. For you. Because what you teach your kids about God will flow out of your own experience with him."

His brown skin and Spanish surname hinted at his Mexican heritage. But it didn't tell his story of growing up in East L.A., one of six kids, his childhood marked by the loss of two siblings. I looked forward to his time with us that morning because his words always conveyed a message of God's pursuit of his people.

Steve handed a stack of purple papers to a mom in the front row. As she passed them out, I looked down at a hand-scribbled diagram with the words "The Critical Journey: Stages in the Life of Faith" written at the top. Steve held up a book and read the title by the same name.[4]

"I don't really like the word *stages*," Steve told us. "It implies chronological order, and these don't have to happen in this order. For me, a lot of things happened out of sequence. I faced tragic loss at age fourteen, so pain preceded my discovery of God. But it was that very loss that helped draw me to him."

I thought of my fourteen-year-old self. I knew my introduction to God's love had been preceded by a life that pointed to my need for a heavenly Father. I've always been grateful that my path to age fourteen made it easier to accept God's hope when I heard it.

Steve began reviewing the stages of our spiritual journey outlined in our handouts. First, the wonder of God—recognizing that he is who he says he is and all the amazement that goes with that. Then the learning phase—often called discipleship—where we learn from others. And finally, service—wanting to put our faith into action, discovering our gifts, and realizing the world needs our contribution. That's where I was when Becca was killed. I was growing, learning, and serving.

"For many Christians, that is where their journey stops," Steve said.

Glancing down at the handout again, I saw that there were three more stages outlined.

"And that can be fine," he continued. "There could be much worse than knowing, learning about, and serving God. But for many, a crisis hits, often around a loss, and they have a crisis of faith."

I looked down again at the violet-colored paper in my hand and saw that the fourth step had a subheading. "The Wall" was written in parentheses on the diagram.

I thought of Becca and the accident. It had been a stopping place for me. Something that knocked my very breath away. I couldn't grasp how God would allow a woman who was creating beauty in the world, loving her husband and her kids, and telling people about Jesus, to be done here. There were so many people making destructive decisions for others or themselves. She was living clean. By the rules. Doing things the right way. And she was not spared.

Pastor Steve went on. "We can get stuck in this stage and stay here forever. Walk away from God. Or we can push through it until we are transformed."

I had to push through that following winter and spring with tiny steps of trust. Figuring out how to help our group process the tragedy gave me purpose in those steps. A reason to get up each day and face the reality that God had allowed this to happen.

While sitting on our guest bed in the basement, holding the phone, feeling as though I'd been punched in the stomach, I'd had an overwhelming sense of a call that I was the person God intended to lead our MOPS group through the tragedy. It feels strange to write that even now, because it could be taken as arrogance, saying that God placed me in that group at that time as the coordinator. Despite my not wanting the responsibility, I knew it was true. I was transformed through leading when I didn't think I could lead. In every task I relied on God to guide my hands and words because I was empty. Rather than *Change me,* my prayer was, *Fill me, Lord. With discernment. With love. With you.* I had to trust he would provide what I needed to lead.

"Once we push through, we are never the same again. We walk with a limp, but the limp becomes part of who we are." As Pastor Steve went through the final step, I looked down at the diagram, and I saw scribbled in his handwriting the final step, titled "The Life of Love."

"You may not care what people think about you as much here," Steve continued. "You've been transformed."

It was true. I had a new sense of God's presence.

For many days after the accident, I thought of Becca every hour. Of what she would be doing if she was still living. If we would have been friends by then. What heaven was like, wondering what she was experiencing. I even talked to her out loud, feeling ridiculous as I did it. "Becca, I didn't know you, but from what I've heard, I would have loved to."

And Steve was right. Though I'd never thought about it in those terms before, I cared much less about appearances. It's as though my priorities were rearranged, and I was grateful for every day my children woke up healthy. Even when I locked my keys in the car. When I had a screaming toddler at a restaurant. When Derek left his dirty socks on the living room floor. None of it mattered. We were alive and together.

And though I could have hit that "wall" and stayed there, questioning God's love for me or any of us, I didn't. I'm not sure why. Maybe because I figured the alternative was bitterness. I knew God was there. I knew he was there when Becca was killed. I didn't understand it. I still don't today. I probably never will. But as my Young Life leader Michelle told me as I was first beginning my faith journey, faith is believing when you still have questions.

Section 10

Fear

i

Prayer

"How are you?" Elisa asked as we walked out of a meeting. I looked at her, and her gaze was sincere. She wanted to know, and I couldn't blow her off, lie, and pretend like life was easy-breezy.

"I'm letting fear have too much control," I answered. It had been months since Becca's accident, and although life was returning to normal by all outward appearances, I knew the details of my decisions were centered in fear. I would call Lindsay from work and ask, "How is everything?" afraid Gabi had pulled boiling water on herself or Genevieve had been run over in the driveway. Every thought went to the worst-possible scenario. I figured if I imagined the worst, especially around my children's safety, I would somehow be more prepared for it.

"Let me pray for you," Elisa said as she followed me to my cubicle. I was grateful for a workplace where prayer was a natural response from a co-worker.

I sat in my office chair, and she put her hand on my shoulder. I don't remember her exact words, but I remember the peace that followed. The rest of that day and then into the next and even the next, I felt a sense of God's presence with me and with my children. Even if I wasn't with them, I knew God was.

The mystery of prayer together. It's sometimes easier, safer, to pray alone in silence. Saying the words out loud commits you to your desires. And articulating them in front of another person is even more vulnerable. What if God doesn't answer them? What does that say about what I want? That it's selfish? Out of God's plan? And yet to have another soul approach God for his mercy on my behalf, as Elisa did in my cubicle, I start to believe it might be possible. Possible that God sees us. Hears us. Knows us. That despite the billions of people he needs to attend to, we each uniquely matter. My brain can't make sense of it, and yet my soul feels it.

I knew it with my girls too. We'd been waiting for days for the tooth to come out. It was hanging and could be twisted in almost any direction, but it was still attached to Gabi's upper gum. The minivan was parked near the front steps of the house, and despite my pregnant belly, I unloaded the grocery bags into the house two at a time. Gabi and Genevieve were wild with energy. It was summer, and they couldn't help themselves—they flung the flip-flops from their feet and ran across the cool lawn from the driveway. Back and forth across the grass, a little bit of country in the middle of their city. Genevieve, who is happiest when her major muscles are moving, threw her head back and laughed as she ran. Her bony legs moved her at rapid speed despite the hot air that surrounded her.

Then the collision. One sister's body parts hit the other's. A whack. A scream. Gabi's hand went up to her mouth. She pulled her hand from her lips and saw blood dripping from her fingers. She quickly looked at me. To see what? That I was close by? That she would be okay? That I saw she was bleeding? Some affirmation of her affliction and some confirmation that she would survive this? She put her hand back up to her mouth.

The tooth—gone.

"My tooth!" Her eyes darted to the grass, searching with desperation. How would she ever find her grain-of-rice-sized tooth amid the jungle of our lawn that, like always, needed to be mowed?

The amount of blood was starting to concern me a little. "Come inside, let's wash you off, and we'll come back out and look for the tooth," I said.

She was now wailing. I couldn't understand what the big deal was, then remembered someone once telling me that during potty training, children can get scared when they poop because they feel like they are actually losing a piece of their body. Maybe the same was true of a tooth for a six-year-old. I tried to be sympathetic.

Gabi turned on the bathroom sink faucet, put her hands under the cool water, and splashed it on her face. As she scrubbed her mouth and chin, her breathing slowed and her sobs turned to whimpers. Little sister Genevieve, who had followed us into the house, stood in the bathroom doorway, not sure if she was welcome to step in.

"We can go back out and look for it. Just get cleaned up." I tried to make my voice sound reassuring, patient, even though I was anxious to get the rest of the groceries out of the hot car.

"I'll help look!" Genevieve's voice sounded hopeful that her sister was ready to forgive.

Gabi lowered the towel from her face and gave her sister a look that said forgiveness wasn't available yet. She turned to me. "Will you pray for my tooth?"

I could feel the pride filling my chest. I really must be a good mom, if this was my child's response to her stress. I gave her my best reassuring smile.

"Yes, of course I will." I sat down on the cool bathroom floor, the weight of my pregnant belly pleading me to sit whenever possible. Genevieve still stood in the doorway, watching, absorbing.

My pride shifted to panic. *Oh no! They really think this is going to work. They think asking God for something will get them what they want. They are believing what I've told them! Do I believe what I've told them?!* I felt I needed to warn them that prayer doesn't always equal desired end results.

Was I really ready to pass on my faith to these girls? Did I believe God enough, trust him enough, to lead my precious babies to him with their heartache, knowing he may not answer their prayers the way they hoped? Did I really believe he heard?

I prayed silently: *God, I'm trusting you on this one*. And then out loud: "Jesus, you know where Gabi's tooth is, and you know how important it is to her that she finds it. We know you want us to ask you, to come to you, with the things that are important to us. Please help us find her tooth." I couldn't believe I was praying for a tooth with such sincerity. I couldn't have cared less about the tooth, but I cared about what this prayer represented to them. To me.

I pushed myself up and walked back out to the front lawn with my expectant girls. They circled the spot we'd left only minutes earlier. Back and forth, much slower now, they walked across the lawn, their bodies bent toward the grass their eyes were dissecting.

"I found it!" Genevieve bent down to the grass and snapped her body back up, her hand above her head like an Olympic champion, holding the lost tooth for us all to see. Confident her big sister would have to forgive her now.

Thank you, Lord, I prayed. I watched Gabi run to her sister, who cradled the precious tooth in her hand. I knew their prayers wouldn't always be answered the way they wanted. My doubts about God hearing and answering made me hesitant to pass on this faith that often felt like it could slip through my fingers. And yet I still believed more than I didn't. In fact, I believed more than ever. I had to trust with them that God heard our every utter. Theirs and mine.

ii

Facing It

Jill is starting a new book group for women from our church. Would you be up for it?

I read Kathy's email and winced. Not what I needed, another thing to add to my schedule. Another program in my life.

Who else is going to be there? I typed back. Kathy and I had maintained our friendship since our MOPS days. I knew it wasn't the question I was supposed to ask—it wasn't supposed to matter who else was part of it—but any nonwork time away from my kids was precious, and I had to spend it carefully. I was easing back into work from maternity leave. Baby girl number three was one more person who needed me. We'd named her Gracelynn. I'd always wanted a Grace, a reminder of God's continued gift of over-the-top love. And we'd planned to give our son my father-in-law's name, Lynn, as a middle name. But at the news of another daughter, we figured it was now or never, so we combined the two for a perfect Gracelynn.

I'd known Jill for years as Kathy's friend, but as our family was settling into our new church where Jill was on staff as an associate pastor, I thought it would be good to get to know her and other women better. Once I saw Cindy was on the list of potential group members, I agreed. It would be good to have a regular place to see both of my longtime friends.

Then the coordination of schedules began. When? How often? I held on to my time like the precious commodity it was. If anything new was going to happen in my life, it had to be when the children were sleeping. Early mornings were easier for me than late nights. We landed on Thursday mornings at six. I would pull out of my driveway at 5:40, in the dark, to get there.

Then the book was announced: *Codependents' Guide to the Twelve Steps*.[5] Codependent? I wasn't really sure what that meant, but I was sure it wasn't me. Maybe it had been at some point in my life, when I was a young, silent woman afraid my boyfriend would break up with me, but I'd changed. I didn't need to spend my precious few hours of social time a week with a bunch of pathetic whiners. And twelve steps indicated this was for people who really had a problem. I considered pulling out, emailing that my schedule had changed and I wouldn't be able to make it. But Cindy said she'd do it too, and I figured most book groups don't really talk about the book anyway.

The weeks that followed reminded me it is possible to make new friends. And I was pleasantly surprised that the book had some actual application to my life. Each week I learned that this wasn't a group of pathetic whiners; in fact, they were the opposite—all capable, mature women. But being capable didn't have to exclude us from hurts from our past. As Jennifer shared about her memories as a substitute teacher at Columbine the day of the shooting, her eyes filled with tears. She had lived with it and "dealt with it" for a decade, but the pain was still there.

Even though Jill didn't want to be the official leader of the group, we all looked to her. She was our pastor, after all. She latched onto my daddy story, or lack of one. I brushed it off. That was my life twenty years ago. It had little bearing on my days now.

"I don't ever think about him," I said. "Besides, I don't even know if he's still alive. It's been at least five years since I've heard from him."

I had birthday parties to plan, preschool snacks to make, and a car to vacuum. I rarely thought about my dad. And why would I? I'd moved on.

Or had I?

That was the question that hung over every angry outburst at my kids, every insecure comment to Derek. Did I have "issues" I wasn't dealing with? Had I shut my heart so tight from fear that concealed hurts were in turn hurting my family? I didn't think so, but I was afraid to dig too far to find out.

We came to Step Four in the book, which was a required exercise, an active examination of multiple hurts or a single thread of hurt in our lives. I felt a tug at my heart—God's nudging, in a sense—that said I needed to revisit the issues around my father. To not let fear keep me from looking at my heart to assess the damage. I resisted. Why would I bring all of that junk back to the surface? It felt as though my wound had been hardened over with scar tissue. Didn't that work? Scar tissue, thick and rough and protecting the open gash.

"I think we should schedule a separate night to review this exercise." Jill moved her eyes around the coffee shop, pointing out the lack of privacy, and then looked around the table to see if we were in agreement. She knew the moms had a harder time sneaking away for a few hours, but we nodded. Yes, we needed more time and privacy than our hour at the coffee shop allowed. We got out our calendars and started the circus of finding a time that worked for everyone.

"What are you going to focus on?" she asked me in front of the group. I didn't appreciate the directness, but she was right to ask, to get us to commit.

"Well . . ." I could feel the emotion rising in my throat. I didn't want to cry or have any feelings about this issue. I was over it.

Wasn't I? But emotion was turning on me, a traitor of my held-together self. It didn't go unnoticed. Jill's gaze became more intent. More intense. And she sat looking at me, waiting for an answer.

"I guess my dad . . ." The tears were now taking over, preventing me from speaking clearly. Me in this codependent support group. "But I'm afraid."

"Of what?"

"Of what might be down there. Stuffed for so long." I was quite aware we had an audience in the other members of the group, but they were kind spectators. Trusted friends.

Jill leaned toward me, her eyes piercing past my face into my soul. "I think it's time," she said. Her words hung in the air, waiting for a response.

I nodded. She was right. I needed to face it head-on. It was time.

I procrastinated completing the exercise until the day before we were scheduled to meet. I prayed for God to give me the courage to feel what had been pushed down for so many years. Though I had lots of friends who were counselors, the only counselor I'd ever seen professionally was the one who did our pre-engagement sessions. And she ended our sessions recommending I do some work. I figured I was in for some serious pain once the floodgates were opened.

I waited until naptime. I made a cup of tea and sat in my living room with a pad of paper and a pen. I started to write free-form. Let the words come out in the order I wanted. And in longhand. That seemed more personal, more primal, than typing on an electronic device. And I waited. I waited to have more to say. To feel more. But there wasn't much.

There was some anger that surprised me. But not a lot. *Where is it, God? I'm ready, ready for the dam to be broken and the floodwaters to come rushing out. Whether they be tears or pain, I can handle it because I know you're here with me. You've always been with me. I'm ready to be honest. Bring it on.*

Silence.

Nothing.

I heard the swish of the water in the dishwasher. Moving. Swirling. And waited for the same in my spirit. It was still.

It turns out that my fear of the pain was mountains worse than the pain that was actually there. I had, in fact, done lots of hard work all of these years and had let go of more than I realized. The pain had certainly shaped me, but it didn't own me. I could be free of the fear it left behind. Now the scar tissue remained as a reminder, almost as a memento of God's redemption of my hurt places.

I heard the baby's cries from the other room. Naptime, quiet time, was over. I closed my notebook and stood up to face the rest of my day.

iii

Plans

I locked myself in the bathroom and took the hidden pregnancy test out of the plastic bag. I'd used the half hour during Gabi's piano lesson to go to our neighborhood Walgreens to buy it. I couldn't have her with me on this errand because she could read, and I couldn't handle the slew of questions my eight-year-old would ask. Her younger two sisters were safe chaperones, though. They had no idea what Mommy was buying at the store.

Dinner was cooking in the oven, and I couldn't wait another minute to take the test. It had to be negative; we were just too planful, too responsible, too unspontaneous for this kind of thing to happen. But there was that one whoops incident a few weeks earlier that gave me just enough room to consider the possibility.

I ripped open the plastic pouch that held the test, a rush of past test-taking memories flooding my brain. As I prayed for the test to be negative, I felt like a teenager.

Two blue lines immediately appeared in the window. I knew this meant I was not only pregnant, I was well on my way in the process. I'd never miscarried; it was safe to assume I was having another baby.

My heart stopped, the beating frozen. How could this just happen? We'd tried for a year to get pregnant with Gracie. I'd had months of disappointing negative tests, and now when I was full to the brim with life and couldn't imagine one more person needing something from me—this?

Gabi pounded out a new song on her keyboard in her bedroom. The notes pushed past the bathroom door, along with Gracie's toddler screams as Genevieve chased her through the house. Their screams were of joy, but they were screams nonetheless, and I wasn't sure I could handle any more noise in my life.

"Whaa?" Derek stood in the bathroom doorway after I sent Genevieve for him. He couldn't even get the question out.

I nodded and started crying. I wasn't happy. I wasn't sad. I was simply emotional. And now on top of that, I was pregnant-emotional. I couldn't believe we were going down this road.

He stepped into the bathroom, shut the door, and stared at me until he finally said, "This is great!"

I knew he was right; I just couldn't wrap my head around it.

The next few weeks, I walked around in a daze. I believe wholeheartedly that God decides when new life is created. I'd believed it from the moment I felt found. I was no accident to him, and neither was this child.

During those weeks, I thought of my mom, imagining her as a single woman with the news of a baby coming. She'd always told me I was a surprise. But she always stressed that she'd been excited, and though I wasn't planned, she loved me. But she must have had other feelings too. Was she overwhelmed? Scared? Apprehensive? I was having those feelings, and I was married and already in baby mode. Though overwhelmed, I realized this unexpected baby would just accentuate the chaos that was already present.

My mom came to visit a few months later. At the dining room table, between water cups spilling and a toddler taking her diaper off, she said, "I had a baby who was a surprise, and she was the best thing that ever happened to me."

I knew this baby was a good thing.

As I folded laundry and loaded the dishwasher, I said many quick prayers for women around the world who were in desperate places. And I thanked God I wasn't. Despite all of my expectations that needed adjusting, I knew I would get to a place of pure excitement and joy for this child. How could I not, with the three complete beauties surrounding me at every turn? And I was not alone. Derek was with me. God was working in my womb. Co-creating a new beauty for me to experience.

At work, I sat in my office and wondered if it was the right time to tell my boss, Karen. I was nervous. I knew she would be disappointed by the pullback this would require in my workload. But I also knew she loved me and really wanted what was best for me. And God had clearly spoken that I was to be a mother of four. I cried as I told her, embarrassed that I was sad about something so precious and miraculous, and also because I knew she was safe. I could tell her I was torn. She would let me feel exactly what I needed to, would journey next to me without judgment, instead offering encouragement for the unexpected ahead.

"I have no idea how much I'll be able to work," I said. She and I both knew that with three kids, I was already saying no to many work opportunities.

"You are a woman with many calls on your life," she said. And then she offered pure wisdom. "Do what only you can do."

I don't know why it struck me as profound, but I knew she was right. God wasn't calling me to do everything. He was calling me to do certain things. And for now that included having another baby.

In the months that followed I repeated that phrase in my head: *Do what only you can do. Do what only you can do.* As questions came up about assignments at work, starting a new MOPS group at our church, activities my kids would be involved in, I asked myself, *Can somebody else do this? What part of this has God uniquely shaped me to take on? If any?* Those questions helped me immediately let go of many things I knew were jobs others could do. I was reminded that what could be a task for me could be a calling for someone else.

And I grieved the plans I'd made for what the next few years would hold: to work more, to have mobile kids who could sit in restaurants and go to movies, to leave them overnight with friends for a weekend away with my husband. Plans that did not include a newborn. As much as I knew what I wanted, I trusted God knew what was best. It was starting to sink in: faith is believing when you still have questions.

A couple of months later, I was getting used to saying it out loud: "I'm having another baby." After three babies, my abdominal muscles were as close to Jell-O as a human body part could get, so I started showing right away and needed to tell the world, and convince myself, that I would be a mother of four.

"Oh, how many do you have now?" a dark-haired woman sitting across from the bar-height table asked me. Her name was Rachel, and we were at a dinner for women from our church. She was new, and I'd seen her around, checking her girls in and out of Sunday school next to mine, but we were really just meeting for the first time.

"Three."

"Oh, wow. We've talked about having a third."

"You should," I said, now a self-appointed recruiter for everyone around us to have more kids so we wouldn't be the lone large family.

"If we're going to, we should do it soon, so there's not too much of an age gap."

Neither of us knew that within a month she would go in for an ultrasound, wondering if she was indeed pregnant, only to be diagnosed with stomach cancer instead.

Section 11

Ten Days

i

Fast and Furious

Baby Giulianna arrived in a fury. The weeks leading up to her delivery didn't seem fast—they stretched out like a summer sidewalk, long and hot. I spent them walking around Denver dilated to four centimeters, wondering what was taking her so long. But when it was finally time for her to come, it was fast and excruciating. Because it was my fourth time around, I assumed my body would know what to do. And it certainly did; I progressed too quickly for the epidural to take effect. I was in and out of consciousness for the hour following her arrival, glad she was my last because I would never want to experience childbirth again after that.

Because she was our fourth, I knew three times over how much I loved her. I knew what was ahead, a love that would change and shape me into a new woman. My experience pointed to the belief. And I trusted it to be true.

My experience also shaped my expectations for the weeks ahead. I knew my days would be filled with nursing the baby and few consecutive hours of sleep. And yet looking at my family's calendar in the four weeks following Giulianna's arrival, I noted two kids' birthdays, my husband's fortieth birthday, and school starting for a third grader and a kindergartner. I cleared my schedule of anything that didn't have to do with those required events. I was going to be smart about it this time and let the first few months be about the baby and my family. Nothing else.

I sat on the chair in the living room, looking onto our front porch as I nursed the baby and scrolled through my emails on my phone. Despite my efforts to minimize, I was attached to the habit of checking my phone anytime I sat still. Through the large windows in front of me, I could see my three big girls playing on the porch. Every few seconds, one would press her face against the glass and cup her hands around her eyes to shut out the glare and make sure I was watching. "See me, Mommy," their motions screamed to me as I watched through the window. "I'm still here, even though you have a new daughter to care for." I smiled through my exhaustion to reassure each one she had a secure place in my heart, and I tried to ignore the fingerprints that were left with each nose-smooshing incident.

Gracie, almost two years old, was leaving a unique nose signature marked with a trail smear of boogies. *She's getting sick,* I thought. *I need to make sure she doesn't touch the baby.* The last thing I needed was a sick two-week-old.

I opened an email from Jill titled "Our Church Family." Only a few sentences, short but shocking. Rachel had died the night before. The blood rushed out of my face. I felt my shoulders slump and the tears flow.

"Derek!" I called. There must have been a strange timbre to my voice because he rushed in the house from the back patio. I couldn't get words out, so I held up my phone for him to read. He bent down and hugged my shoulders while I cried.

The girls came rushing in from the front porch. "What's wrong, Mommy?"

How do I explain this? I thought.

"Mommy's friend Rachel died," Derek answered.

"You mean Jane's mommy?" Genevieve asked. Her eyes widened as she thought of her friend from Sunday school.

"Remember how I said she was sick?" I asked through my tears.

Genevieve nodded.

"She didn't get better."

Genevieve turned and ran down the hall to her room.

I'd been out of the Rachel loop. While I was delivering sweet new life, Rachel was coming to the end of hers. She took a turn for the worse, with her last few days in a coma. The progression at the end went at the same speed as the rest of her cancer: fast and furious.

I was left right back where I'd been with Becca, asking, *Why, God? Why this mom?* Only this time, she didn't just leave a grieving husband, she left two little girls. I was sure God would spare her. Her girls needed her. And not in a petty "I really need a bigger kitchen" sort of way. Their lives, their hearts, would be changed completely by their mother's death. And she was such an incredible mother.

I felt the baby pressing down on my arm that cradled her and remembered only months earlier when Rachel wondered about having another baby. How was it that I came to have this baby, this new life, this blessing that I didn't ask for, straight from the life maker himself, and she died? Another tragedy to add to the list of things I would likely not understand this side of heaven.

I was one big hormonal, wet, drippy mess. And my heart was broken. I called Cindy. I was sure she'd heard, but I wanted to make certain she knew.

"I was there," Cindy said.

"What?"

"I was with her. I was with her when she died."

"What?" My brain couldn't get what she was saying. I was still in shock that Rachel had been as sick as she was, but Cindy had been with her as she moved from one place to the next. From this world to forever.

"After she died, I pulled her oxygen tubes out and told her, 'You're free now. You're free from the pain. From the suffering. You're free.'"

I pictured Cindy, her long blonde hair pulled back in a ponytail, using her training to release Rachel's body from the tubes that tried to keep her alive. Second nature for a nurse to deal with the tubes, her years of practice kicking in, yet so against her nature, her understanding of how the world works, to watch a friend, a fellow mom, leave this world early. Cindy then went home to her family plus two little girls who had stayed for a sleepover.

"I pushed them on our swings this morning," Cindy said, "and thought, *She'll never do this again. Rachel will never push these girls on swings again.*"

I pictured Rachel lying in the hospital bed and wondered what that transition was like. Moving from the tangible to beyond. What was she experiencing now? Could she see her girls? Her husband? Was she in God's presence? How did that feel?

The next morning we managed to herd our now family of six into the minivan and to church. I was grateful for an hour of Sunday school and nursery for my big girls, trusted care that gave me a break and let me sit in the sanctuary with the baby snuggled up. But it was more than the free child care. I wanted to be there. With my community of believers. My shared place with Rachel.

During the announcement time, Jill said Rachel's family was coming to Denver from California and Nevada for the funeral. I thought of our basement with its three bedrooms, a bathroom, and a kitchen. The college girl who lived with us all summer had just moved out, leaving plenty of private space for a big group that wanted to be together. I told Jill after the service it was available.

A few days later, Jill brought over an air mattress. Kristi gave me extra towels. I bought snacks and drinks to stock the basement kitchen. I hadn't been able to be with Rachel when she was dying, but maybe I could give her family a comfortable place to stay. I cried as I picked up toys in the playroom. Praying for God's presence in that space in the days to come.

I knew nothing about the people who would arrive. I was only sleeping two hours at a time, and I could feel my throat starting to get scratchy. Had Gracie gotten me sick? It didn't matter; I was alive and Rachel wasn't. I could do this. I would do this. I would love her in this way. I made beds with the baby strapped to me in the bjorn.

Do what only you can do. My home and my heart had been positioned to offer this to her family. The "do what only you can do" was not only about cutting things out of my life, it was also about stepping up when it was time.

ii

At My End

I pried my eyelids open. Was she really ready to eat again? It felt like I'd only been asleep for a few minutes. I heard car doors slam through our open bedroom window and thought how different our neighbors were from us, coming home at 2:30 in the morning. I was seeing a lot of 2:30, but that was by force of a hungry baby. Then I heard a rustling and more slamming of doors. I sat up, climbed on my knees to look out the window above the head of our bed, and saw two figures dressed all in black going through a car trunk on the other side of the street. Strange. They didn't look like the neighbors I was expecting, but I didn't know everyone on our block. Then one of the figures shut the trunk, and they both ran without a sound to the next car on the street.

I now know what it is to have a shiver go down my spine. I watched as one slid a small object down the doorjamb of the second car. He quickly unlocked the door and popped the trunk. The car's interior light went on, and I could see the partner going through the glove compartment on the passenger side while the street-side thief ran back to evaluate the trunk's contents. Within seconds they were shutting doors and running on to the next vehicle. Thieves in the night. Sinister and silent.

I shook Derek and whispered, "I think someone's breaking into cars." After calling the police, we discovered our cars, which were parked in the driveway, with the doors open and our garage door up, but nothing gone. I knew right away that they broke into our cars and then used the garage door opener to open the garage.

I stood in my pajamas knowing they'd been there only minutes earlier. Two faceless figures there to rob us, to take what was rightfully ours.

"They were probably looking for easy things to pawn," Derek said, the light from our garage spilling out into the darkness of our driveway. I guessed his table saw was not an easy item to carry away.

We whispered in the hall, not wanting to wake the houseguests filling our basement, in town for Rachel's funeral. It wasn't until the next morning that we realized the sound that woke me was the smashing of Rachel's father-in-law's minivan window. They stole his GPS. *Why not just stab this family in the heart and then wriggle the knife around a little?* I thought.

The day before the funeral was spent filling out police reports and calling insurance companies. I couldn't shake the sinister nature of the night before. Evil. The opposite of good. I knew it existed. The counterforce to love. With the visual of two silent figures slithering through our neighborhood, I felt it in a palpable way. Dark. Mysterious. Making people do awful things. Letting cancer take over a young mother's body and take what was rightfully hers—a life with her family.

The days followed with the funeral, hugs good-bye to new friends, and Cindy's family coming over for dinner. We'd had an exhausting week, but theirs had been even more intense. I couldn't remember ever feeling this drained. I figured it was traumatic childbirth followed by sleep deprivation combined with hormones and grief. Cindy held Gracie on her lap and wiped her boogies. I was thankful for friends who found comfort in being together.

The next morning I took pictures of Genevieve on her first day of kindergarten. My second girl going to all-day school for the first time. Proud, excited for her, and sad the baby years were slipping away, I was starting to feel manipulated by the emotional extremes of the last two weeks. That afternoon was my first naptime with two at home and two at school, so I finished revisions for a work project that was past due. As I typed, I started getting chills. It was inevitable, I was getting whatever Gracie had.

The next day I couldn't move. The chills were more extreme. I was shaking as I held the baby. Standing up and walking into the kitchen occurred to me, but I couldn't make my body follow my mental instructions. I mustered enough energy to push the play button on the television remote for another episode of *Dora the Explorer* for a worsening Gracie. I watched the digital minutes tick away on the television's cable box. Every minute a minute closer to Derek's return from work.

The next morning I woke up and knew I needed to see a doctor. I made back-to-back appointments for me and Gracie and kept the big girls home from school. They were showing signs of getting sick too.

Carol called to check on us. "I'm coming with you to your appointments," she said. It sounded nice to have another grown-up be in charge, but I knew it would take her whole afternoon to drive down to our house, spend two hours at the doctor's office, and then drive home, so I declined the offer.

"You can't do this with four kids," she said.

"I have to. I will always have four kids," I snapped into the phone. I was keenly aware that this was the beginning of the rest of my life. A simple chore like going to the doctor sounded exhausting, but it was my new reality, and I needed to figure out how to manage it.

"But you won't always be sick." She was gracious with my snapping, and she was right. I was sick, and help sounded wonderful.

Thankfully she came, because six hours after our phone conversation, I was leaning over Gracie in an ambulance, transporting her from our doctor's office to Rocky Mountain Hospital for Children. I'd been diagnosed with pneumonia, and Gracie's oxygen levels were low enough she needed to be hospitalized.

The Tylenol I'd taken before we left our house for the doctor was beginning to wear off, and I could feel the shakes starting again. My breasts were bulging with milk, but the baby wasn't allowed in the ambulance with me. Carol was driving my other girls to our house, where she'd meet Derek. He would then bring the baby to the hospital, though it would be a few hours later. This new reality of four kids was requiring a military-strategy map, and my brain was too fuzzy to quickly think through it all.

Derek and I had our reunion in an ER exam room. I was shaking from the chills, Gracie was screaming from the tubes in her nose, and the baby was screaming her tiny baby chirps from hunger. I slapped the baby onto my breast and tried to talk over Gracie's screams to come up with our family-management plan for the next twelve hours. Gracie was being admitted for pneumonia. The nursing baby took me off the list of staying at the hospital, so Derek was on for the night duty. It was already late in the evening, and I knew the older two girls would be waiting for me to get home before they'd fall asleep. I wasn't sure I had enough energy to drive myself home, much less meet everyone else's needs.

I put my face close to my daughter's and said, "Gracie, I love you," and willed myself to turn around and walk out of the ER with her screams at my back. I was certain I'd never felt more torn to be in two different places. A scared Gracie needed me to comfort her. The baby needed my breast milk with its antibodies to protect her from the germs swirling around our family. My older girls, scared from their sister's ambulance exit and also starting to cough, needed the reassurance of their mommy at home.

Driving home with the baby in her car seat, I stopped at a red light and laid my head on the steering wheel. I wasn't sure I could make it the next twelve minutes to our house. I prayed, *God, I have nothing left. I am empty. All I have is you.*

Five days later, Gracie came home from the hospital. Five days of feeling pulled in two different directions. Of wanting to meet all my kids' needs and unable to do it. Five days of depending on my mother-in-law to be with a screaming Gracie, restraints on my daughter's arms to keep her from pulling out her tubes. Five days of my friends rotating shifts at the hospital to walk the baby around the lobby so I could give Gracie some undivided attention. Five days of pneumonia-induced body aches and wet pillowcases as I cried myself to sleep, picturing Derek squished on the hospital sofa and Gracie in the hospital bed with tubes in her nose.

When she came home, it felt as though I'd experienced the greatest endurance test of my life. And I passed—barely.

iii

Phone Call

The day after Gracie was released from the hospital, Crystal came over to help me organize the chaos that had taken over my house. We cleaned out the fridge in the kitchen and the extra one in the laundry room. Half-eaten casseroles that had been dropped off two weeks earlier by new baby well-wishers were tossed. I pulled back the silver foil covering a few and decided I wanted them all gone. I wanted a fresh start.

The house phone rang, and I stepped away from the fridge to answer it.

"Hello?"

A long pause.

"Uh, hello?" I heard the woman's accent on the other end. This was either that frustrating respiratory therapist from the hospital—the one who couldn't explain how to use Gracie's inhaler—or Europe calling. "Is this Alexandra?" she asked.

"Yes." I was annoyed, remembering what a poor communicator the respiratory therapist was. I didn't have time or energy to deal with her. I was done with the hospital.

"Uh, Alexandra Kuykendall?" she asked.

"Yes." *Let's get on with it,* I thought. *I have a lot of lost time to make up for, and Crystal is only here for half an hour more.*

"Uh, I'm calling to tell you . . ." Another pause. I was starting to think this wasn't the respiratory therapist. This was Europe calling.

"Uh, your father . . . died."

I glanced over at Crystal washing the crisper drawer in the sink.

Really? I thought. *Now? This week?* I pressed the phone to my ear.

"He died this afternoon."

With the time difference, I knew that was probably seven hours earlier. I was surprised that she, the mother of my younger sisters, was calling. And so soon after it happened. I was more surprised by the prompt call than I was by the message.

What was I supposed to say? I hadn't known if he was still alive, so I wasn't really shocked by the news he was dead. *I should say something,* I thought.

"Was he sick?" I asked.

"I'm sorry. My English is not very good." Her accent was heavier than I remembered. "He was sick for . . . uh . . . ten years. . . . He could not say many words. . . . But he said your name. . . . Over and over he said, 'Alexandra. Alexandra.'"

I could hear the grief in her voice. And maybe some nervousness about calling me to break this news. I wanted to be sensitive to her sorrow, but I couldn't mirror it. I didn't want to offend her, but I was completely numb. I had nothing to give back. Nothing to say.

"We will have a funeral here . . . in France . . . in two days. Maybe someday you can come to visit."

I pictured the church in the center of their town and wondered if that's where he'd be buried. I couldn't remember if there was a cemetery there.

"Here is your brother," she continued. "His English is better."

I glanced over at Crystal again. She'd abandoned her post at the sink to soothe squabbling kids in the living room. Their little voices had transitioned from playing to arguing, and she was trying to mediate. I walked out of the kitchen and into the laundry room, shutting the door behind me. Shutting out my current life to step into my past for a brief minute. *Really? Today, God? This is all happening today?*

"Hello?" I heard a man's voice. My brother. We hadn't spoken since Derek and I were in Barcelona twelve years earlier.

"Hello." I looked around the laundry room, thinking, *Now what?* Moving from one room to the other hadn't helped. It was still awkward, and I still didn't know how I was supposed to respond.

"Our father . . . he has died."

It sounded dramatic. Maybe it was the accent. Maybe it was getting a phone call from France telling me my long-lost artist father had died. It sounded like something you'd read in a novel. The mountain of laundry on the floor next to the dryer felt more tangible, more real, than anything having to do with this conversation.

"He had a heart attack . . . but not of the heart . . . of the brain," he explained.

Oh, a stroke.

We spent the next few minutes catching up on the past twelve years. He has a daughter. I have four. Our conversation was brief. He asked if Facebook was the best way to reach me. I said it was.

They'd thought of me. The most shocking part of all was they'd thought of me.

I walked back into the kitchen to find Crystal back at the sink, scrubbing the crisper drawer.

"My dad died." I knew how dramatic it sounded, but after the week I'd had, it felt good to say something dramatic.

Crystal stood frozen, her body half turned from the sink, the dish brush in her hand. Without taking her eyes off me, she reached over and turned off the water. "Are you okay?"

"I am." I couldn't believe how okay I was. I knew coming off the last week, I was as empty as I'd ever been. But shouldn't I be feeling something? "Maybe I'm just numb."

"Okay, well, sit down." I could tell she was searching for the appropriate response. I was too.

"No, I'm okay. Really." I couldn't shift gears. I was focused on cleaning out the fridge. *We should keep working,* I thought. Like my friend Erica, whose water broke when she was making a coffee cake for a brunch that morning. She couldn't adjust her day's plan; she just kept making the coffee cake.

"Are you sure? Tell me what happened." She was searching my expression, trying to read where I was, but my poker face wasn't offering any clues.

"I haven't talked to him in years. I didn't even know if he was still alive."

"Well, do you want to go? To . . . where did he live?" She crinkled her brow. I knew she was trying to remember.

"France. No. I have no reason to go. And after the week we've just had, I'm not going anywhere. They don't need me there. I just can't believe they called. And so soon."

I bent my legs to sit in the chair overlooking the front porch. I didn't want to sit but felt tired. Breathing was still difficult.

"I can't believe it happened this week."

Gracie ran into the room, followed by Crystal's son. Despite the oxygen cannulas taped to her cheeks, she was laughing. The tubing for the oxygen tank connection dragged behind her, disconnected from the tank, not needed until sleep time. Numb and exhausted, I looked at Gracie and I smiled.

iv

I'M OKAY

When are you coming home? I texted Derek. Crystal had just pulled out of the driveway, late to pick her older kids up from school.

Why?

I have to talk to you.

What?

I'll wait until you get home.

My phone rang. I didn't have to look to know it was him.

"What is it?" He sounded both worried and annoyed. We'd just had ten days of accumulating bad news. Neither of us was comfortable with speculation.

"I really need to tell you in person," I answered. I knew he was irritated, but this would take more processing than he could squeeze in between work appointments.

"I'm really behind. I don't know when I'll be home. Just tell me."

"I'm okay. The girls are fine. I just want to see your face when I talk to you."

I knew he'd understand when he found out what it was. A few hours later, sitting on our back patio, I could tell he did.

"How are you feeling?" His voice softened.

"Nothing. I'm feeling nothing. I didn't even know he was alive, so I don't know, I guess I'm okay."

He nodded. He knew better than anyone that I'd already grieved. I'd spent my life working through this loss. This just meant any chance at a relationship was over. But I'd made that decision the last time I'd said good-bye, when Derek and I pulled out of my father's gravel turnaround driveway.

"I think it's significant that he kept saying your name over and over."

"I know," I said, "it probably is." But I didn't know how. Guilt? Regret? Hope for final words? Someone could have called me, held the phone up to his ear, but they didn't. If there was something more he'd wanted to say, I would never know.

"Maybe I'm just exhausted. Maybe I have nothing left to feel right now. Maybe it will come out in ways I don't expect."

I spent the days that followed trying to put order back in our family life after ten days of crisis. I took Gracie to doctor's appointments, threw a fortieth birthday party for Derek, helped a kindergartner with her separation anxiety, and attended to my month-old baby. But physically, I wasn't getting better. I still felt like all life had been sucked from me, and I would sit down often. Even standing to make peanut butter and jelly sandwiches was exhausting. *So much for an empty schedule,* I thought. But I was grateful I'd built that time margin into those first few months. I went back to the doctor and got another round of antibiotics.

Then one day I sat on my sofa and googled his name. I wondered if there'd been any press on his death, so I went looking for it. Following trails, I attempted to decipher newspaper articles in Spanish and Catalan. They all focused on his work. None mentioned any family.

I felt as though I'd found some treasures, and I wanted to call someone. Someone who would understand their significance. But I had no one to call, at least nobody who understood the journey

I'd been on, who'd experienced it with me. My mom had been there, but she saw things from her perspective. *Normally someone would call a sibling,* I thought. I could call Derek, and he would love me through it, but not really understand. Understand what it's like to read my father's obituaries in foreign languages, with no mention of my existence. I felt alone.

But God knew. He'd been there at every point. From my conception forward, he was my traveling companion. He knew my backstory as well as I did, but beyond that, he knew the joy that would come. Much of my life I felt I was walking on unsteady ground, hoping that where I chose to place my feet would somehow make me more secure. And yet here I was with the husband, the children, the job, the church I'd dreamed of, and nothing about the last few weeks hinted at security. Things that made no sense to me, things that caused me to call out to God in fear, still happened. My only stability was Jesus.

I could not, would never, be able to control my circumstances. The one thing I could count on was God. He created me. He loved me—the plain-old-housewife, mother-of-four me. I know in many ways I'm ordinary. Not too different from millions of other women. And in just as many ways I'm extraordinary, woven together by my unique biology, circumstances, and choices. A unique reflection of my Creator.

After the initial shock and "I'm okays" I offered concerned friends, I wondered if I really was. Was I really okay with this most recent turn of events—that my father was gone? And I decided I was. I'd closed that door many years ago. I'd peeked behind it a few times to make sure it was all good. And it was. But more, it was knowing that when stripped to my core—when I had to lay my head on my minivan steering wheel, not sure I could make it home—I called to God for help. When I had nothing left. No energy. No words. Not even prayers. God was there. He was my only real security and the definer of my soul.

Epilogue

My Inheritance

Scrolling through the email inbox on my phone, I froze: an email with my father's name as the subject. It had been two months since the phone call with news of his death, and I'd heard nothing. This isolated conversation echoed of the girl who found a letter in the mailbox with familiar handwriting and foreign stamps. The possibility of what could be, but never was, written inside. Words that indicated potential for a relationship, for a father's love, and then—nothing. Silence, forgotten again.

I pressed my finger on the phone's screen and found a letter written in French. Like with the handwritten letters of years past, I skimmed through the words searching for the significant, but quickly realized my Spanish wasn't going to help me with French as much as I thought it should. I did make out enough to know it was from a lawyer and had to do with my father's estate. Normally emails like this are spam: a long-lost relative in a foreign country has died. But my unconventional life led me to know this was for real.

In the days that followed, I worked at translating the letter, using a conglomerate of Google translate, my boss who had just returned from vacation in Paris, and Kristi's high school exchange student. What I pieced together were words that sounded cold, distant, impersonal. The opposite of personal, of a person—me. Did I want to assert my position as his daughter? That's what it appeared to be asking. Really? After all these years, I was the one with the burden of proof? This brought more grief than the news of his death. This question once again of where I fit. Where I belong.

Was it the translation that made it sound so cold? The legal language? The nuance was impossible to discern. No voice inflection. No body language to read. Just words on a screen, asking, "Are you his daughter or not?"

Days later, more emails arrived, but now with attachments. I opened them, and my heart skipped as I found my father's familiar handwriting. Longhand letters that took me back to my girlhood. I reviewed them over and over, trying to make out both the handwriting and the language, searching for something. Something that said he loved me.

They were makeshift versions of his will with different dates, all from years earlier—one in Spanish, one in French, and one in Catalan—but only one of the three mentioned me. Did this mean he thought of me a third of the time? Or I had a third of the value of his other children? Why did I even care after all these years? I'd moved on. Hadn't I?

References to God's inheritance in the Bible flashed to my mind. I'd never really paid attention to them; the language seemed antiquated and irrelevant. Now I had new clarity. God mentions inheritance for a reason. Inheritance, what we get when our father dies, speaks to our value in his eyes. I knew I'd read it in the Bible somewhere, but where? I found Ephesians 1:11 (NLT), where God says, "Furthermore, because we are united with Christ, we have received an inheritance from God, for he chose us in advance, and he makes everything work out according to his plan."

We are united with Christ. I'd felt his sacrifice. With every burden I carried, every grief lived, I felt closer to Jesus, who took on the burdens of the world. Every moment I loved my children, my husband, my mother, I better understood his love, united with him more closely with each passage.

We have received an inheritance from God. His promise not of an easy life but of a life everlasting. Lasting ever. Forever. Together with him.

He chose us in advance. It's true I'd felt chosen by God. Picked out of the crowd and known. Ever since I'd felt found, I knew I was no accident to him.

He makes everything work out according to his plan. Not that he planned it all, but he uses it all, he makes it all work for his purpose. Not mine. Not ours. Not the thief in the night's. But his.

Days later, I received another email in my inbox. It was from my older sister. A surprise, but something I'd been hoping for, something less formal, more personal, without lawyers. She had typed and translated our father's handwritten, makeshift wills into Spanish so I could better understand them. She wanted to know if I was okay with fulfilling his wishes. I could now see with certainty that I was mentioned in only one of the wills. The other two, not at all. That my siblings could choose what artwork I received, if any. The sting burned more intensely than I expected that they had so much power in determining my value. I wanted my father to see me as his, and this felt like I was an afterthought. Like a secondary citizen.

Part of me wanted to fight. To stand up and shout, "This is rightfully mine! *This!* This title of *daughter*. I will not be ignored anymore; I will get what I deserve!"

Interesting hearing those words in my ear: "get what I deserve." Because none of us do. That's the gift of grace. None of us deserve

God's love, and yet it's what he left when he died. An inheritance of forgiveness. Of acceptance. Of love.

Mostly I just wanted the whole situation to disappear. Dealing with it sounded exhausting.

"What should I do?" I asked Derek.

"Do you feel like you need to be recognized as his daughter? Is there something in you that needs that acknowledgment, separate from any money?"

"I don't think so." And despite those pangs of hurt, I really didn't. "But this doesn't just impact me," I said. "Should I be fighting for something on behalf of our family? For our kids?" Really I meant, should I be fighting for money? Did I owe it to Derek and the girls to push for something that could help our family?

"You don't want to fight." Derek's look reminded me he knew me better than anyone. "And it's not like we've been counting on any money."

That was true. I loved my husband. He wanted what was best for my heart and not our checking account.

"What I really want is for them to hear me. To say I'm here. I've always been here."

"Then say it."

He was right. My sister's email was asking for a response, giving me a chance to confess my life's hurts. To say things that had gone unsaid for a lifetime. And maybe I was finally ready to say them. I didn't need an inheritance of money because I had an inheritance of grace. I hadn't understood that earlier—as a girl, as a college student, as a newlywed, as a new mom. But I'd grown, matured, in confidence of who I was. Of who defined me. I could say what I needed to without fear of the consequences because my inheritance of grace was permanent. I could and would cash in on that.

I took my laptop into our bedroom, closed the door, and sat on the floor, my back against the wall. From where I was sitting, I could see myself in the full-length mirror. My eyes. So much like my father's with their piercing blue and the dark circles underneath. But there was more than genetics staring back at me. I saw in them a life journeyed, with more still to go. These eyes looking back were starting to have creases on the side. Wrinkles? I wasn't ready, but those hints at wrinkles told a story. My eyes had seen a lot. *What will they look like thirty years from now? What will they have seen?* I wondered.

Looking back at the computer and the empty screen, I slowly inhaled. I was supposed to be good at written communication. But this required a level of crafting I wasn't used to. Cultural and language differences, family dynamics, and history called for straightforward, concise verbiage, but I wanted those words to echo my desire to love my afar family despite our years and miles apart. To extend grace from my grace-soaked heart.

Despite all of the constraints of language and awkward circumstances, I tried to let the words flow freely. I attached a picture of me and Derek and the girls sitting on our front porch earlier that month. I ended with these words:

> *Although this is a matter of the estate, please know this is also a matter of the heart for me. I have felt forgotten by my father much of my life. I cannot replace what I longed for so much as a girl—a relationship with my father. I have made no efforts in recent years to contact him. I decided after my last visit it was too painful, and I needed to move forward with the family Derek and I are making.*
>
> *I ask that you remember me in this process, if nothing else, to symbolize a shift in the legacy left. I ask that you not forget me, but recognize that I am also his child.*

I hit the send button and looked up at my reflection in the mirror, thankful. I didn't have to worry about the response because I was found before I realized how lost I was. Thankful my inheritance was grace everlasting. That I didn't have to wait for it or fight for it. It was now. Not because it was rightfully mine, not because I had to prove my position, but because God, the artist of all things true and beautiful, loved me, called me into existence, claimed me as his daughter, and never left.

But me he caught—reached all the way
from sky to sea; he pulled me out
Of that ocean of hate, that enemy chaos,
the void in which I was drowning.
They hit me when I was down,
but God stuck by me.
He stood me up on a wide-open field;
I stood there saved—surprised to be loved!

God made my life complete
when I placed all the pieces before him.
When I got my act together,
he gave me a fresh start.
Now I'm alert to God's ways;
I don't take God for granted.
Every day I review the ways he works;
I try not to miss a trick.
I feel put back together,
and I'm watching my step.
God rewrote the text of my life
when I opened the book of my heart to his eyes.[6]

Questions for Reflection

Section 1 Insecurity

Barcelona

1. What was your relationship with your father like? Your mother?

2. Describe a moment when life didn't meet your expectations.

Italy

1. What childhood experiences shape who you are today?

2. Where did your eight-year-old self imagine she would be today? How is it the same? How is it different?

Apartment

1. When have you wanted more from something or someone?

2. How did the place, the culture, you grew up in impact your understanding of the world?

Zoo

1. When have you had to hold feelings in?

2. When has a hurt come bursting out? How did it feel when it finally did?

Section 2 Love Is a Choice

Jesus

1. When was the first time you heard about Jesus? What was difficult to believe? What was easy?

2. What influenced the way you understood him?

Boys

1. How did your childhood impact your understanding of boys and men?

2. Who were your role models for marriage, if you had any? How did they impact your thoughts on marriage?

Perfection

1. Do you struggle with performance or perfectionism? If so, who are you trying to impress? If not, what motivates you to do well?

2. How did or do your parents respond to your achievements? Do they still influence how you make decisions today?

Choose Me

1. When have you failed to get someone else's attention? How did that feel?

2. How do you define love?

Section 3 Trust

Trajectory

1. If given the chance to do anything, how would you react? Would you feel freedom? Would you be paralyzed? How would you decide your next steps?

2. Have you ever felt God's prompting? If so, describe the experience. If not, would you like to? What would you need to sense his prompting?

Impressions

1. Describe a time when you have been vulnerable with others. Did it feel risky? Safe? Why?

2. How do you decide when it's time to hold it in and when it's time to share?

Secrets

1. Has anyone ever shared a painful secret with you? How did you react?

2. How do you make sense of God when terrible things happen?

Surrender

1. When has trusting felt risky?

2. When have you surrendered to trust?

Section 4 Legacy

Fights

1. When have you expected someone to meet your needs?

2. How did you balance your expectations with the reality of what the other person could offer?

Heroes

1. Are there beautiful and ugly parts to the legacy your ancestors offered? How do you manage those?

2. What parts of your family history would you like to pass on to your children as a legacy?

Forgiveness

1. When has forgiveness felt like a challenge?

2. Do you think forgiveness is more about you or the person you are forgiving? Why?

Section 5 Motherhood

Pregnancy

1. How was your adjustment to pregnancy and motherhood? How did it differ from your pre-mothering expectations?

2. How have you fit into the family of your child's father? Has this changed since becoming a mother?

Delivery

1. Describe your entrance into motherhood through birth, adoption, or marriage. What did it feel like in those first few moments? First few days?

2. Did you have an instant connection with your child? How did you grow in your understanding of your role?

Hormones

1. Have you ever suffered from mood disorders due to hormones or depression? Were you able to realize it at the time? If so, describe that time.

2. What is your current support system? Has it always been this way?

Rocking

1. Has being a mother impacted your understanding of your own parents? If so, how?

2. Has parenting impacted your understanding of God? If so, how?

Section 6 Friendship

Longing

1. What is it like for you to make new friends? Are you naturally able to connect to others?

2. Do you ever feel alone in a crowd? If so, what things help you connect with others?

Comparisons

1. When have you compared yourself to someone else and fallen short?

2. What assumptions could others make about you based on appearances? Would those assumptions be correct?

Judging

1. When do you find yourself judging others? Why do you think those moments are your triggers?

2. Do you consider yourself a rule follower? Does that make it easier or more difficult to know Jesus? Why?

Section 7 Coming into My Own

My Baby—Myself

1. Do you feel like you are an extension of your mother? Why or why not?

2. Do you feel your child is an extension of you? Why or why not?

O Christmas Tree

1. Were there parts of parenting you dreamed about? If so, what were they? How did your dreams compare with real life?

2. Do you sometimes "forget to remember"? What helps you remember?

Daddy's Girls

1. How do you parent with your child's father? How do his personal qualities and strengths show up in his parenting?

2. When have you expected someone to do things like you would?

Retreat

1. In what ways do you seek affirmation?

2. How does the knowledge that no parents are perfect impact your understanding of your parents? Of yourself as a mother?

Section 8 The Main Thing

Anger

1. What makes you angry in a given day? If you are not sure, track it.

2. When do you find it difficult to keep the main thing the main thing?

Change

1. When have you successfully implemented a heart change in your life? How have you done that?

2. Has a difficult experience ever been a catalyst for change in you? If so, how?

The Right Way

1. Have you ever changed your mind on a strongly held belief? If so, what prompted that change?

2. What part of your daily routine makes your soul sing? How can you add more of that to your life?

Section 9 The Accident

Headlines

1. When have life circumstances caused you to ask, *Why, God?*

2. Have you ever wanted someone else to take over as the grown-up in your life? How did you press forward?

Grief

1. How have you held up in a crisis? What helped you cope?

2. When has someone's death impacted you? How did you make sense of it?

The Wall

1. Where would you place yourself in the steps described in this chapter?

2. Have you pushed through a wall? Have you been transformed? If so, what does that look like?

Section 10 Fear

Prayer

1. When are you afraid? Do you pray when you're scared?

2. Do you have difficulty trusting God with people you love? If so, in what area?

Facing It

1. When have you faced a fear? What was the result?

2. Describe a time when you've been surprised by your feelings or your reactions.

Plans

1. When have you been afraid of God's blessings?

2. What can only you do?

Section 11 Ten Days

Fast and Furious

1. When does life seem unfair?

2. When have you seen God's goodness and life's hardships at the same time?

At My End

1. When have you reached your end? How did you cope?

2. What or who did you find was left when you had nothing?

Phone Call

1. How easy is it for you to shift gears when life requires it?

2. Describe a time when you were surprised by how well you handled something. What does that say about you, the circumstances, and your growth?

I'm Okay

1. Do you believe God sees you and knows you? Why or why not?

2. What defines your soul?

Epilogue My Inheritance

1. Do you think you will ever "arrive"? If so, under what circumstances? If not, why not?

2. Do you consider yourself God's daughter? Why or why not?

Acknowledgments

There is no way to thank everyone who shaped this book. It would require thanking anyone who has ever shaped me, and there aren't enough pages. So I keep my acknowledgments to those who had a role in this writing project.

Thank you to my mentors at MOPS International for believing I could tell my story and it would matter. I especially thank those who read and gave feedback. Thank you to Carla Foote for prayers that moved my heart when I desperately needed them, to Elisa Morgan for reading every word and modeling leadership and risk, and to Carol Kuykendall for your storytelling expertise and love language of Words of Affirmation.

Thank you to the team at Revell for taking on this new author with enthusiasm. I appreciate your skill in the world of book making. A special dose of gratitude to Andrea Doering for "getting me" and this project like no one else could.

To MOPS leaders everywhere, thank you for giving me daily inspiration to love other moms with courage and generosity. You motivate me to give past the comfortable. I thought of you and the women in your MOPS groups as I wrote every word.

A huge thank-you to my five at home. Among soccer practice, hospital stays, and "what's for dinner" questions, you looked past the mess of the house so I could deal with writing down matters of the heart. To Derek for the hours of listening to written words read aloud and the ideas, feelings, and questions that surrounded them. I love you forever.

Thank you to my friends and family who were included in these stories. You had no idea as we did life together that I would one day record it in this way. I realize I tell these stories through my lens, and you give me grace to do so.

Thank you to God my Father, the grace giver, who gave me my very breath. I give my story back to you.

Notes

1. Psalm 119:176.

2. Philippians 3:2, 7–8.

3. Philippians 3:9.

4. Taken from Janet Hagberg and Robert Guelich, *The Critical Journey: Stages in the Life of Faith*, 2nd ed. (Salem, WI: Sheffield Publishing Company, 2004).

5. Melody Beattie, *Codependents' Guide to the Twelve Steps* (New York: Touchstone, 1992).

6. Psalm 18:16–24.

Alexandra Kuykendall lives in Denver, Colorado, with her husband, Derek, and their four daughters. She is on staff at MOPS International (Mothers of Preschoolers), where she is a regular contributor and consulting editor to *MomSense* magazine, *Connections Magazine*, and MOPS video curriculum. Her writings can also be found on the MOPS blog and in various devotionals, including *Daily Guideposts: Your First Year of Motherhood*. While she spends most days buckling and unbuckling car seats and trying to find a better solution to the laundry dilemma, she manages to snatch minutes here and there to write about the quest for purpose in it all. Connect with her at AlexandraKuykendall.com.

CONNECT WITH ALEXANDRA ON

@alex_kuykendall

alexandra.kuykendall.5

Alexandra Kuykendall

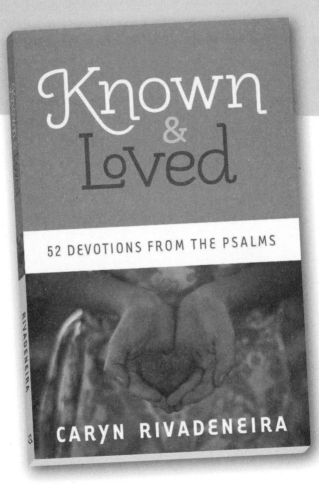

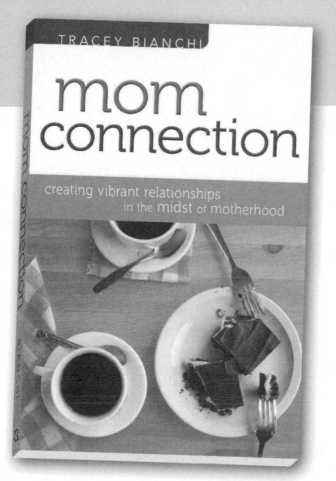